Thank you for completing our qu

ANIMAZING
TOYS

better for children, parents and the planet

www.animazing.toys

Please read and share this book

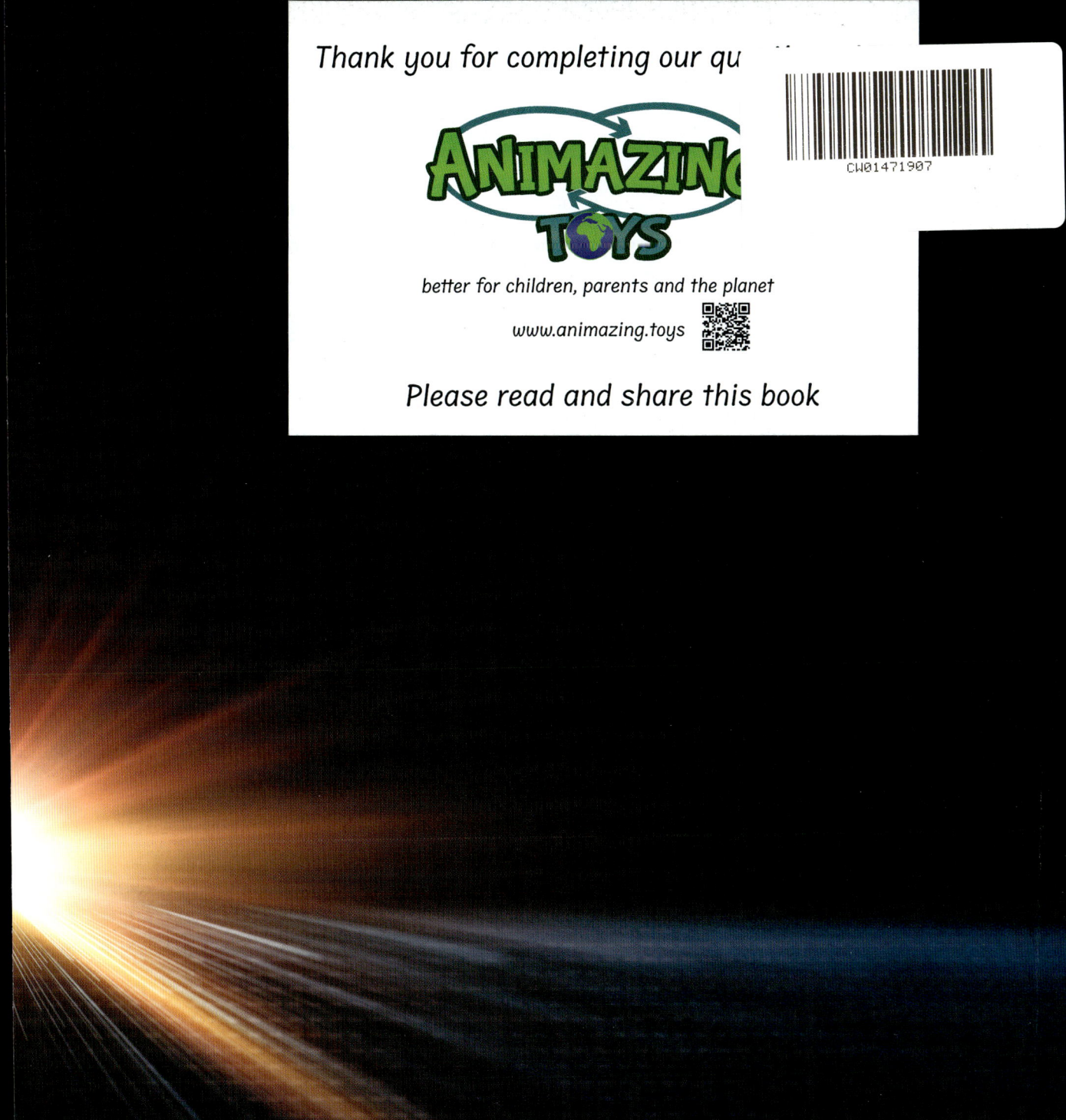

DISCOVER
COMPUTERS & CODING

First published 2022 by North Parade Publishing Limited
3-6 Henrietta Mews
Bath
BA2 6LR, UK

Predominant artwork and imagery source: Shutterstock.
Additional images: David Smee

Contents

The History of Computing

Why did we invent computers?

The word *computer* was first used in the 1600s to describe the job of people whose work was to calculate numbers. We now understand computers to be electronic devices that offer much, much more than just mathematical calculation but, as we'll show you, it's exactly that challenge that has made computers what they are today. Can you believe that the human need that drove us to create computers might have started 35,000 years ago? Evidence exists that Neanderthals painted lines on walls which experts have interpreted as the first counting marks. These might have helped cave people share out buffalo or keep track of the number of people in the village, it's very difficult to tell as we are talking about a very, very long time ago!

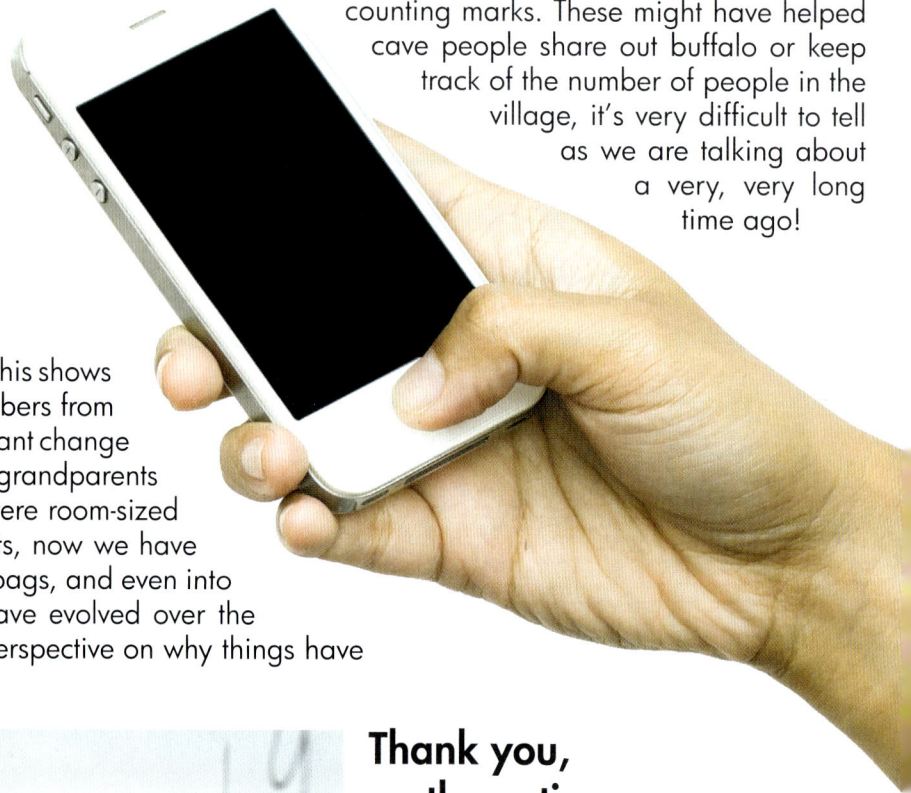

The cave painting evidence is significant as this shows humans wanted to record and display numbers from our earliest times. However, the most significant change for computers has happened since your grandparents were born. Just 60 years ago computers were room-sized machines used only by a handful of experts, now we have far more powerful computers that fit in our bags, and even into our pockets. As we explore how things have evolved over the next few pages, it'll help give us a useful perspective on why things have turned out as they are.

Thank you, mathematics

Calculation of numbers and more recently spreadsheet software to automate calculations, has been vitally important to computers' success. It's worth realising that if people hadn't wanted to improve our ability to do maths, we probably wouldn't have computer games. When you next head into your maths lessons, just think of all the positive technology innovations that started with maths! Going back to our historic timeline, after cave paintings, the next stop on the journey to the present day is 20,000 years ago, when Early Man scratched notches on animal bones to help keep count. These are considered to be the first forms of tally marks: a way to visibly count things (like money, livestock or any item of value) which became commonly used across the globe right up until the 19th Century.

Tally Stick

The word *tally* came from the Latin name for a stick. It was the wooden form of tally mark that dominated for centuries. This was mainly because writing materials such as papyrus and parchment were far too expensive for most people. Paper started to be used around the 14th Century but tally sticks remained popular for counting. To 'tally up' is still used today (mainly by older folks) as an English expression that means to add up, for example, some shopping items "Can you tally that up for me please?"

The Abacus

The first portable calculating machine invented is the abacus. You may well have already used one of them yourself to help learn how to count. They consist of moveable beads or counters in a series of rows or columns, allowing you to add in single and multiple units (as you can see in the image below). The word *calculate* comes from the Latin word for *pebble*. *Abacus* is understood to have derived from the Hebrew *abq* meaning *sand*, before it became *abax* meaning *counting table* in Greek. It seems logical that stones and marks in sand aided calculations before those pebbles were drilled with holes and mounted into wooden frames, to create this enduring calculating system.

Abacuses were popular in Greek times but are understood to have first been used at least 2500 years before this, about 5000 years ago in Mesopotamia (which had the famous city of Babylon, an area in southern Iraq). The idea was such a good solution that it passed through Ancient Egypt, Persia (the Middle East), China and Russia to be popular worldwide to this day.

The First Computer

Even two thousand years ago, amazing mechanisms were created – firstly by the Greeks - using movement in cycles to calculate time and the movement of stars, as seen in the Antikythera mechanism (100BC) and then the Al-Jazari programmable clock (1206) from Turkey. These early analogue computing mechanisms helped pave the way for mechanical calculators as automation and the engineering of smaller and smaller metallic mechanisms continued to improve.

Mechanical calculators

It took until 1623 for Wilhelm Schickard to conceive the first mechanical calculator using Napier's bones. These were numbered strips (see image below) published by John Napier in 1617 that helped simplify multiplication and division based on a technique now known as lattice multiplication.

FACT FILE

An algorithm is a finite set of instructions that, when followed line by line, solves calculations or performs other computing operations.

Schickard's idea didn't work reliably when put into a machine, so his design never become a product that people could buy and use. The credit for the first working mechanical calculator is given to Blaise Pascal, who solved the weaknesses in Schickard's design and created the Pascaline to simplify the calculation of taxes in 1642. Napier's Bones were also the basis for the slide rule (1622) an essential maths accessory for children right up until the pocket calculator became more widely available in the 1980s. Count yourself very lucky as calculators are so much easier!

From calculators to the first computer

The mechanical calculator innovations that started in the 17th Century, alongside the steam-powered machines developed during the industrial revolution (1760 to 1840), set the scene for Charles Babbage's invention of what we now recognise as the first programmable digital computer. A great deal of what he conceived in his work still exists in computers today.

Charles Babbage (pictured right) lived between 1791 and 1871 and, being from a wealthy family, was well-educated, allowing him to develop significant talents across a range of topics. His favourite subject and the one he pursued for a Cambridge University degree was mathematics. During his time at University his attention and imagination became focused on finding a way to reduce human errors in complex calculations. Initially, it centred on a specific calculation he believed he could automate.

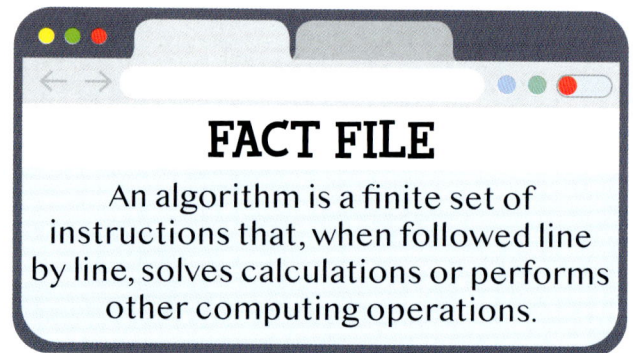

The Difference Engine

Babbage's first innovation (1822) was an automatic mechanical digital calculator, named his *Difference Engine*. This was because the mathematical principle on which it was based is called the method of *finite differences*. His idea was a mechanism that calculated polynomial functions at the crank of a handle. Polynomials have multiple algebraic terms with constants (like 8), variables (like x or y) and exponents (like x2), so plenty of separate parts and lots of opportunity for calculating errors. Solving a polynomial like this f(x) = 9x3 + 2x2 − 4x +13 is daunting to most people. He believed that if a machine could be used to simplify the calculation of polynominals, you wouldn't need to employ a maths genius to solve the problem and it should be right every time.

Only a section of the Difference Engine was sold to the Br<i>i</i>stish government during Babbage's lifetime. The challenge to build it completely was too great in his day. It took another 169 years (1991) until the Science Museum in London constructed a fully working version, you can see it there now. It isn't exactly a pocket calculator, the complete machine weighs approximately 4 tons and stands about 8 feet tall - a huge mechanical monster!

The Analytical Engine

After his father died in 1827, Babbage was left a sizable inheritance – the equivalent of £8.5million in today's money, meaning he now had significant resources of his own to help him invent. When development on the Difference Engine stalled, principally due to Babbage's disagreements with engineers, he set to work on a more ambitious project. Rather than solving a single mathematical challenge, he next wanted to create a programmable calculating machine. First described in 1837, his Analytical Engine design has four core components still used in computers today. The enduring aspects were:

1) Being programmable – it could work on different problems using punched cards

2) Having data storage – it was capable of storing 1000 numbers to 40 decimal places

3) Using a calculating "mill" - the equivalent of a processor (CPU) where calculations were performed

4) Output devices – printing answers out on a plotter or on punched cards

The First Programmer

Ada Lovelace (1815-1852) had a brilliant mind and, like Babbage, was a talented mathematician from a wealthy background. Having been introduced to Babbage as a young lady, she was intrigued by his calculating machines and their potential. Babbage recognised her talents including an awareness of the latest scientific developments. He asked for her help to describe the function and potential for the Analytical Engine. Using notes taken by an Italian engineer that, being multilingual, she was able to translate, she annotated this description with her own vision for this invention that went far beyond just numbers and calculation. In her work, she described how codes for Babbage's Engine could also manipulate letters and symbols. She also created the first computer algorithm to automate complex calculations. Lovelace was also the first person to propose a 'looping' process to repeat a set of instructions to a machine even before machinery and weaving looms had started to use them. Her ideas were an inspiration to Alan Turing and his ground-breaking work on computers in the 1940s. Lovelace is now considered as the world's first-ever computer programmer.

Computers in the 20th Century

The electronics industry began at the turn of the 20th Century, triggered by the invention of the vacuum tube by John Fleming in 1904. Vacuum tubes (known as valves or tubes) act as diodes in electronic circuits. A diode's purpose in electronic circuits is to manage the direction of the flow of electric current. This means it can be switched on or off or regulate how much current passes. Diodes were used as switches and amplifiers in almost every electronic device including radios, televisions, telephones and sound systems for decades.

This time (1900 to 1950) became known as the 'Vacuum Tube Era' and gave rise to the first generation of computers. During the 1940s priority was given to computer development for its potential to give an advantage to win World War II. Vacuum tubes were a key element within world-changing computing innovations in this period, especially for code-breaking computers including the Bombe and Colossus.

Software starts

Computing software (by that we mean programmes stored in computer memory and run on the computer's processor) began in 1948 with the creation of the Manchester Baby. Prior to this, programmes were external and fed into the computer itself, loaded as punched cards for example, which Herman Hollerith, a founder of IBM invented. It took decades for software technology to mature and before it became commonplace to have a computer's system software preloaded inside. If you look at the companies whose core business is software today, like Facebook, Microsoft and Google, they are among the most valuable companies that exist on the planet. In the past 30 years, software has arguably created the most significant changes in human behaviour in the shortest period of time and those three companies mentioned have played a significant part in that. Before all this happened, in 1935 the concept of computer programming and ideas of a general-purpose computer that began with Babbage and Lovelace, led Alan Turing to develop the theory of software in a now world-renowned essay Entscheidungsproblem (decision problem).

Turing is considered to be the father of modern computing and artificial intelligence for his vision and development of computing at this early stage. His idea of a general-purpose processor central to a computer and controlling all data manipulation became known as the 'Turing machine'.

FACT FILE

Binary, that is numbers expressed only as 1s and 0s, is the basis for all storage, transfer and manipulation of data in computing systems. Binary is what the computer understands in language terms and is the basis of machine code, the language that Computer Processing Units (CPUs) read.
Boolean numbers also have one of two possible values, typically true or false, and form the basis of computing logic.

The Colossus (1943) invented by Tommy Flowers used binary code strings loaded onto the computer in complex ways, using punched cards, switches and plugs. Flowers worked alongside Alan Turing, whose focus during the war was (famously) cracking Enigma coded messages using the Bombe computer. Recognised as the first programmable electronic computer, Colossus was an outstanding achievement. At the time of its invention, the most sophisticated electronic devices used about 150 thermionic valves, but in order to decipher complex codes more quickly during World War II, the Colossus used 2,500. It weighed 5 tonnes and needed a large room and a lot of engineers to operate it. Yes, it was massive in every way – hence the name. Today, a device that fits in your hand would have more computing power and be far more reliable than the Colossus was.

Five years earlier in Germany, mathematics genius, Konrad Zuse had created a computer we now know as the Z1. This was the first binary electromechanical programmable computer ever. Amazingly, this was done using his family's savings and was assembled in Zuse's parent's home. Next time you have a wonderful contraption taking up space around your house, you may want to mention to your Mum or Dad that inventor Konrad Zuse's parents let him use their entire living room for a whole **2 years** from 1936 to 1938, in order to build the first electromechanical programmable computer!

Computing Innovations (1940 to 1980)

1942: the first electronic digital computer, the ABC (Atanasoff-Berry Computer).

1946: the Electronic Numerical Integrator and Computer (ENIAC) was the first general-purpose, *fully programmable* digital computer. Many consider this the first real computer.

1947: the first computer powered by transistors. Transistors replaced vacuum tubes due to their better reliability, size and cost. Transistors made from silicon are now microscopic in size - thousands of times smaller than the width of a strand of hair! Millions of transistors are used in microprocessors – single silicon chip CPUs – found inside all computers today.

1948: the first computer runs on software stored in its electronic memory (Manchester Baby).

1949: the first graphical computer game called "OXO," an implementation of noughts and crosses as it's known in the UK (tick, tack, toe in the US) displayed on a 6-inch cathode ray tube.

1950: Kathleen Booth developed Assembly Language to make it easier to programme computers.

1959: COBOL created by Grace Hopper as a data processing language for business use.

1962: IBM creates System/360, a family of computers that could run the same software apps + Sketchpad – the first programme to use a graphical user interface (GUI), revolutionising human-computer interaction. Sketchpad is seen as the origin of computer-aided design (CAD).

1964: BASIC (Beginners' All-purpose Symbolic Instruction Code) initially developed to broaden the appeal of computing beyond 'science & maths' became the default programming language for mini and microcomputers.

1971: Intel introduces the first microprocessor, a single chip CPU (the 4-bit 4004).

1974: the first successful microcomputer, the Altair 8800 made by MITS and based on the Intel's 8-bit 8080 CPU. The 8800 was ordered from magazines and sent to customers in kit form to make themselves.

1975: Bill Gates (see image) and Paul Allen (the founders of Microsoft) write the Altair BASIC compiler.

1977: Apple II designed by Steve Wozniak and Steve Jobs (see image opposite) made PCs relevant to home use and opened the door to software for consumers. Visicalc (1979) for Apple II was the first spreadsheet (maths) programme for PCs and sold over 1 million copies, many to businesses.

1980: IBM offered Microsoft the opportunity to develop PC-DOS (aka MS-DOS) for its new IBM personal computer, which was based on ideas like expansion slots, taken from the Apple II.

FACT FILE

Silicon is a semiconductor used in all computers today. Only oxygen is more abundant on Earth than silicon; it is the main element within beach sand. Semiconductors act as an insulator (they stop electricity running through them) until you alter their conditions, then it switches into being a conductor.

The last 40 years

We could finish the book by just listing the many computing innovations of the past 40 years; instead, here are some of the most significant themes from each of these four decades.

1980s – home personal computers and business laptops emerge

By the 1980s personal computers were changing from self-assembly hobbyist kits, to become more conventional products that you'd find in many electronic retail shops. The Commodore 64 (1982) still is the most popular PC ever with up to 17 million sold. The IBM PC 5150 (1981), the Apple MacIntosh (1984), Sinclair Spectrum and Amstrad CPC 464 were other important models of the period. Laptop computers were starting to take shape within businesses with products from IBM, Epson and Micral. Keyboard and mouse inputs were swapped for joysticks or gamepads in the emerging sector of games consoles, led by the Atari 2600 and then Nintendo's NES.

1990s – games consoles and mobile phones for all

Sony had originally been working with Nintendo to develop new gaming products. After the partnership broke down in 1992 Sony was determined to succeed with their own product. Their PlayStation consoles took gaming to new heights, the first version (now known as PS1) launched in 1994 and sold over 100 million units. Their second console, the PS2 is still the most successful console ever, selling 155 million units. Although the PlayStation ruled the 1990s, Microsoft's Xbox360 and Nintendo's Wii proved to be strong alternatives in the 2000s. Console wars between these three continue today. In parallel, PC gaming has remained a strong format in its own right and gaming on phones is now the most popular of all. Led by Nokia and Motorola, mobile phones were changing from being only just portable (briefcase-sized) to ones that could fit in your pocket. The first text message was sent in 1992, heralding the start of mobile data and Internet.

2000s – dotcom beyond the bubble & Smartphones apps launch

In the late 1990s, the Internet had already caught the world's imagination. Even before companies had proven any ability to deliver revenue, large financial investments were made in the latest dotcom …anything! This created a financial bubble that burst (meaning money was lost). However, the early investors had helped build the foundations of the Internet success that was to follow for the likes of Amazon, Google, Facebook and eBay. Smartphones had also started in the 1990s as a way of business users having access to their work 'anytime and anywhere.' In 2007, the Apple iPhone with touchscreens for fingers rather than stylus pens and mobile apps helped bring smartphones to the masses. Nowadays mobile apps allow you to do just about anything you can do with computers.

2010s and beyond – content in the cloud and coding for all

In the last decade, we've eradicated the need for tangible forms of storage for films, books, music and work tools – everything can be stored digitally and downloaded or streamed from the cloud. This has heightened the importance of cybersecurity as important information might be stolen if someone hacks into the right server. The surge in 'digitalisation' has come to a point where the focus is now on how we can democratise the ability to create software. Everyone can learn to code digital apps, websites and products. This book gives you extra knowledge to complement what is taught in school, with a little bit of computer science theory mixed in with real-world coding skills.

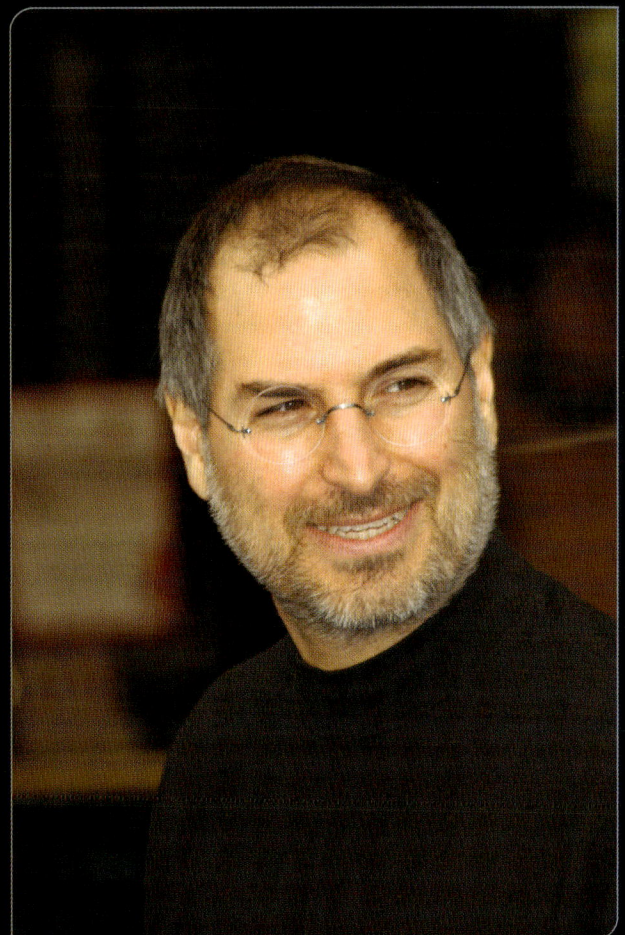

The Physical Elements of a Desktop Computer

The physical elements of a computer are called its hardware: basically, anything you can touch is hardware. The input and output devices that plug into a computer are hardware called peripherals, we'll look at examples of those here. One very important input device is the keyboard. The keyboard layout below is called QWERTY due to the top line of letters, highlighted in red below. This is the arrangement best suited for typing words in Latin-based languages such as English.

The 'Home Row' is the line of keys where your fingers should be resting when you start to type, your left index finger on F and your right one, on J. The backspace or delete key is always near the top right of the keyboard, so you don't press it by accident.

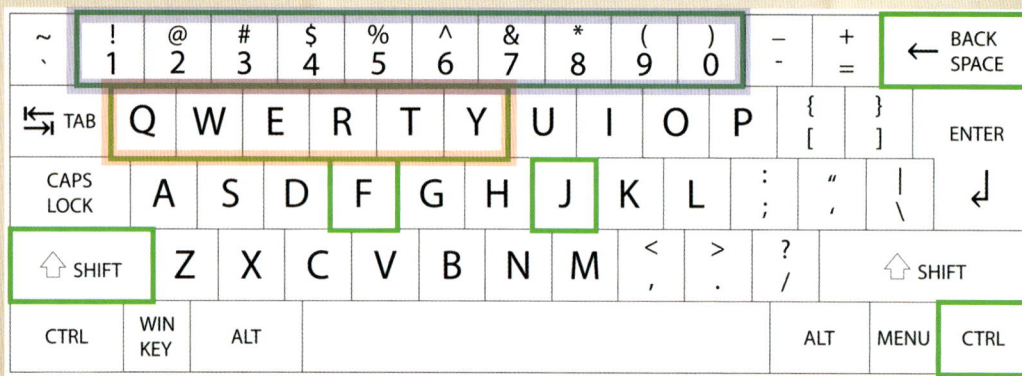

This is th
cursor:

It's
controlle
by the
user's h
moving
mouse.

Holding the 'Shift' key down allows you to capitalise the letters on the keyboard, but also, importantly for us, to use the extra characters and symbols on the numerical buttons (top row, highlighted in blue). These characters are used a lot when you write computer programming languages (code).

Examples of output devices

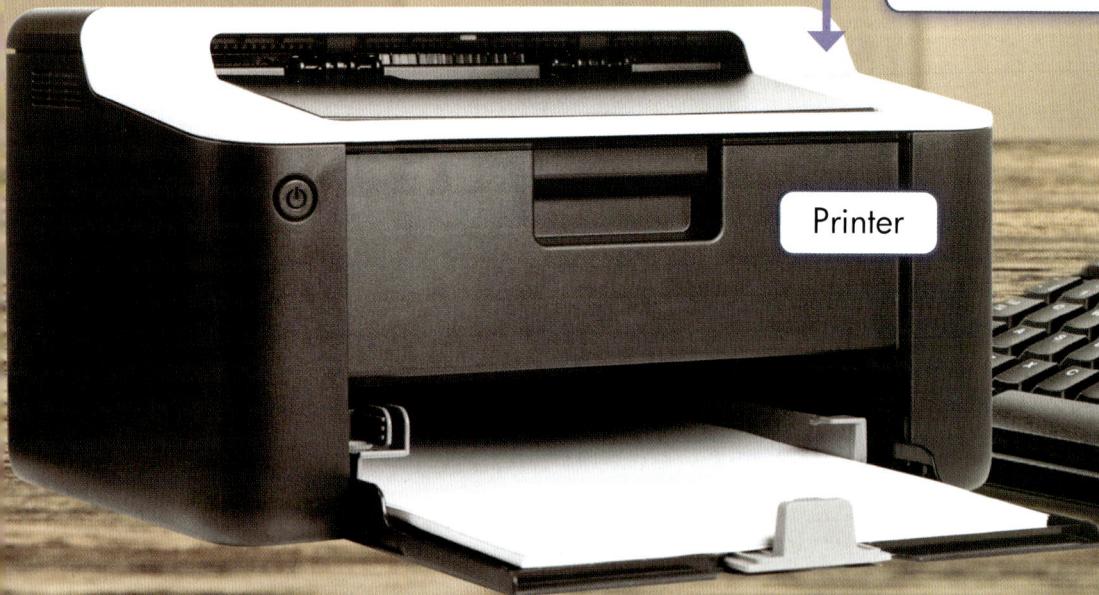

Printer

Keyboard

The desktop tower contains the 'guts' of the computer including the CPU, which we will explain further on the next pages

Desktop Tower

Monitor

The cursor can move all around the screen and enables you to quickly arrive at the exact place you need to be, for example in a document or a page of code.

Laptops do much the same thing using trackpads. Touchscreens don't need cursors as you use your finger to interact directly instead.

The left mouse button allows you to click on buttons or links on the screen

The right mouse button gives an extra set of selectable options in a drop-down menu

Mouse

Examples of input devices Keyboard, mouse

What's Inside a Computer?

To simplify the computer, we've shown it in block form. We mentioned Charles Babbage earlier and the parts of a computer he invented with his Analytical Engine. You can see the parts he created (Input, CPU, Memory and Output) still exist in the layout below. The user's experience is what we as users see and how we interact with the computer. Our experience relies heavily on the system software that determine the user interface (UI) and programmes that can run on the computer (see page 20).

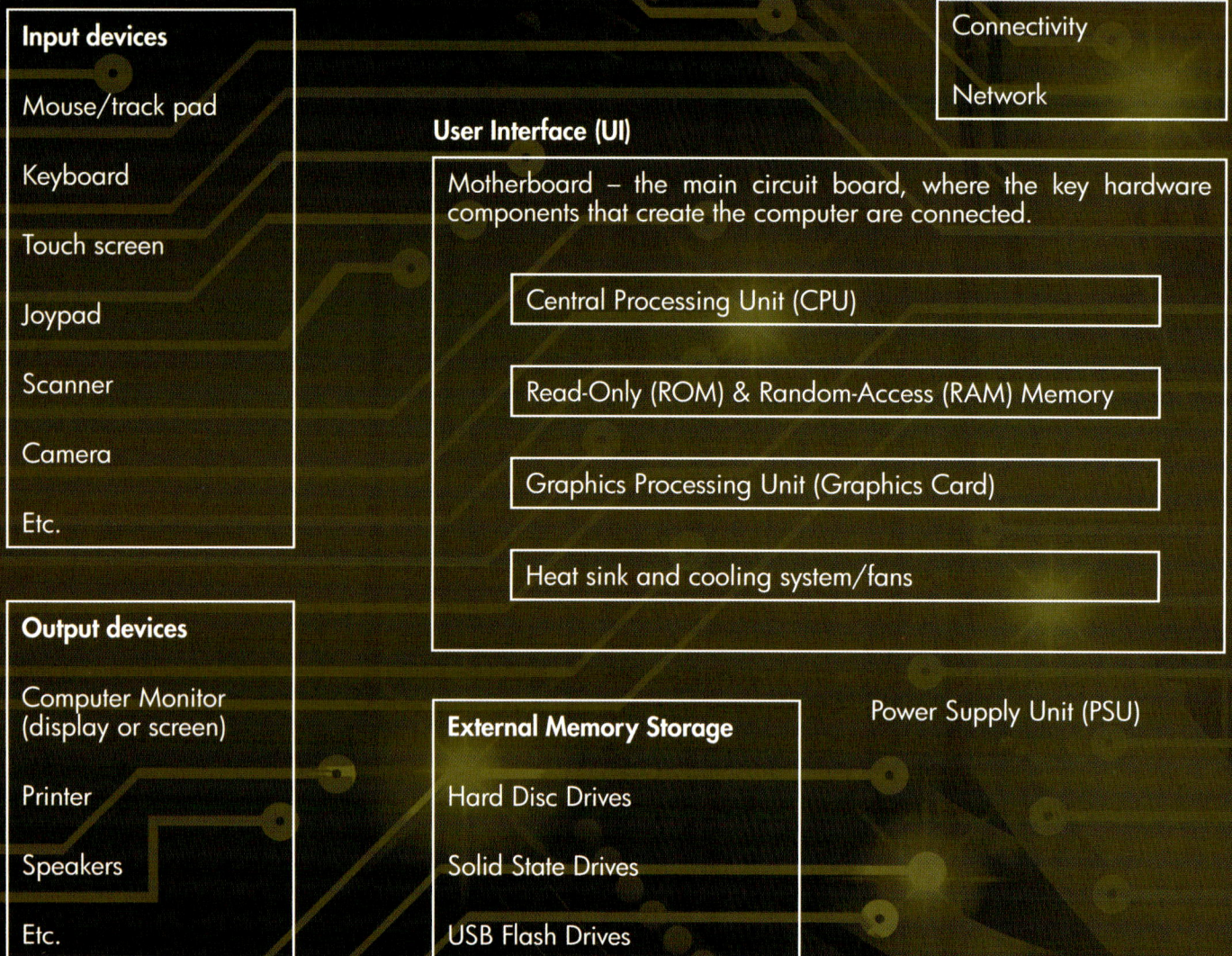

Input devices

Mouse/track pad

Keyboard

Touch screen

Joypad

Scanner

Camera

Etc.

Output devices

Computer Monitor
(display or screen)

Printer

Speakers

Etc.

Connectivity

Network

User Interface (UI)

Motherboard – the main circuit board, where the key hardware components that create the computer are connected.

Central Processing Unit (CPU)

Read-Only (ROM) & Random-Access (RAM) Memory

Graphics Processing Unit (Graphics Card)

Heat sink and cooling system/fans

External Memory Storage

Hard Disc Drives

Solid State Drives

USB Flash Drives

Power Supply Unit (PSU)

Data is transferred through the computer's components using 'system bus architecture'. Originally these were parallel interconnecting wires, nowadays they can be any type of electrical connection, most commonly pins or tracks on a printed circuit board (PCB). PCBs are green boards inside the computer where electronic components are mounted, the motherboard is the main PCB. The system bus connects the CPU to the memory and the inputs/outputs (I/O) on the motherboard. The separate buses within the system bus are the Control, Address and Data buses, which allow the different signals and data to be sent around the motherboard under the control of the CPU.

Inside the CPU

The Central Processing Unit (CPU) does all the hard work in the computer. It is essentially the computer's brains making all the decisions and calculations using data and instructions. The CPU is generally described in 3 main parts: the Control Unit (CU) which manages instructions inside and controls the CPU, the Arithmetic Logic Unit (ALU) which performs the calculations inside the CPU, and the Cache. Cache is very fast memory either inside or just outside the CPU itself, faster than RAM but not as fast as the registers (see below).

In 1945 John Von Neumann – another mathematician and an early computer scientist – proposed the architecture (blocks of functions) shown below, which describes a system where the CPU runs programmes stored in memory. It still describes how most general-purpose microprocessors work today.

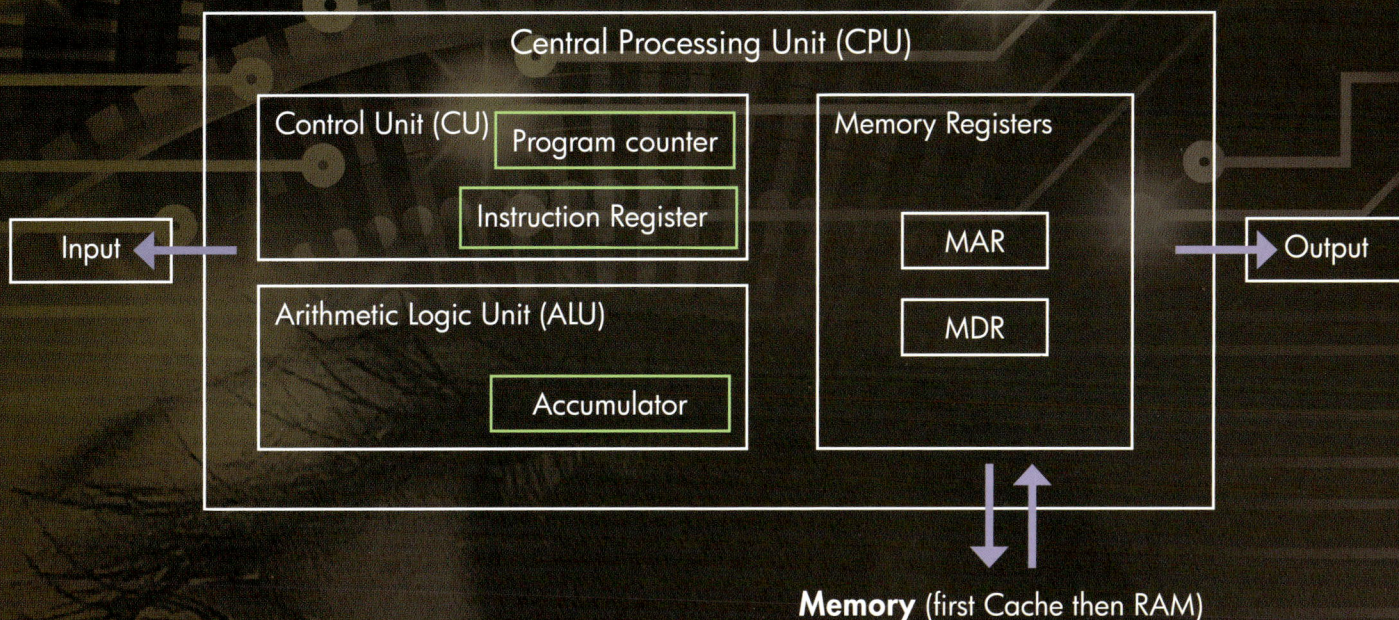

```
┌──────────────────────────────────────────────────────────────────────┐
│                    Central Processing Unit (CPU)                       │
│   ┌────────────────────────────────┐   ┌─────────────────────────┐     │
│   │ Control Unit (CU)              │   │ Memory Registers        │     │
│   │   ┌──────────────────────────┐ │   │                         │     │
│   │   │ Program counter          │ │   │                         │     │
│   │   └──────────────────────────┘ │   │    ┌──────────────┐     │     │
│   │   ┌──────────────────────────┐ │   │    │ MAR          │     │     │
│   │   │ Instruction Register     │ │   │    └──────────────┘     │     │
│   │   └──────────────────────────┘ │   │    ┌──────────────┐     │     │
│   └────────────────────────────────┘   │    │ MDR          │     │     │
│   ┌────────────────────────────────┐   │    └──────────────┘     │     │
│   │ Arithmetic Logic Unit (ALU)    │   │                         │     │
│   │   ┌──────────────────────────┐ │   └─────────────────────────┘     │
│   │   │ Accumulator              │ │                                   │
│   │   └──────────────────────────┘ │                                   │
│   └────────────────────────────────┘                                   │
└──────────────────────────────────────────────────────────────────────┘
```

Input ← │ Output →

Memory (first Cache then RAM)

The Von-Neuman Architecture explains the function of a CPU in three steps:

Fetch an Instruction -> Decode the Instruction -> Execute the Instruction

This process is known as the fetch-decode-execute cycle and repeats until there are no more instructions.

The CPU has a range of registers within it that hold very small amounts of data for a very short period, they operate at unfathamable speeds. This is how the fetch-decode-execute cycle works with the registers:

The **Program Counter** holds the memory address of the next instruction that needs to be fetched from the memory. Let's say that instruction address is 1234. Cache memory is searched before RAM.

The contents of 1234 is then transferred to the **Memory Address Register** (MAR), which holds this information for a fraction of a fraction of a second before the **Control Unit** sends a signal to fetch it. 1234's instructions are held in the **Instruction Register** within the CU and data is transferred along the data bus to the **Memory Data Register** (MDR). This is the end of the fetch part of the cycle.

Decoding is performed in the CU, splitting the instruction into command and address. The command is executed in the **Arithmetic Logical Unit** (ALU) using the MAR, MDR and Accumulator to store address and data information. The resulting data is transferred to the address in RAM that the command (stored in the MAR) was instructed to write to. This completes the fetch-decode-execute cycle and should help you understand how dynamic CPUs are if billions of these happen every second. It's not surprising they can get quite hot during use!

Computer Performance

The main factors affecting a computer's performance relate directly to the CPU. These are the processor's clock-speed, its cores, memory and their connections, which need to be comparable with each other to deliver the best performance. Generally speaking, a high-spec computer should make everything you use run faster and more smoothly than a lower-spec one. However, other factors including available bandwidth for online programmes and glitches in software can create the impression of poor performance. That's to say, if you have the most high-spec computer in the world and a very low bandwidth connection to the Internet, you probably won't be able to enjoy an online game experience as much as someone with a better Internet connection even on a low power computer.

Clock Speed

Every CPU has a clock which co-ordinates all the computer's components. The speed of its electrical pulses are the CPU's, and therefore the computer's, **clock speed or clock rate,** measured in Hertz (Hz). Hertz is a measure of frequency, meaning the number of instruction cycles per second the processor can manage. Each instruction carried out by a processor is, in itself, a simple calculation but when done at supersonic speeds, the performance delivered gives the impression of great intelligence. The faster the calculations, the smarter the computer seems. Today's computers have CPUs which range from entry-level ones with around 1GHz (that is 1 billion instructions per second) to very high-performance

FACT FILE

Electromagnetic waves were discovered by German physicist Heinrich Hertz in 1883. If it helps, you can remember "Herz" in German means "heart" in English, which beats approximately every second.

processors running at 5GHz. These are commercially available computers. Industrial **supercomputers** can go way beyond this, but you pay a lot for even small increases in performance within them. The Commodore 64 in 1982 had a processor speed of around 1MHz (1 million instructions per second), so even today's basic computers are a **thousand times** better than your parents' generation!

Processors can be **overclocked** to increase their performance; this means their settings are altered through the BIOS (basic input/output system) software to run beyond the levels that the manufacturer had chosen them to be used at. This can make them run hotter than usual. Cooling is, generally, another important factor for computers as components become smaller and more powerful. The main ways this is achieved is by using fans, heatsinks (materials that redirect heat) or liquid cooling.

Core

A computer can contain one or more CPUs, these individual units are called **cores** and can act in parallel with each other to increase a computer's performance. During the past 20 years increasing cores has been an easier way of improving computing performance, mainly due to heat dissipation issues within the minuscule silicon strands. Computers often have dual (2) or Quad (4) core processors and with them can run multiple programmes and apps at the same time. However, as cores need to communicate with each other to work, doubling the number of cores doesn't actually double the speed of the computer.

Data Bus

Buses are circuitry that move control signals and data around the computer. The data bus's task is to process data between the main memory and the processor and it is bidirectional. The control and address buses are both unidirectional. Increasing the size of the data bus improves the system performance. A 64-bit data bus transfers double the amount of data (per second) of a 32-bit one.

Cache and RAM Memory

The **Cache** (pronounced cash) is a small amount of memory typically within the CPU itself. If the computer can use cache memory this is the fastest way to process information, so a bigger cache is better for processing speed. 8MB is currently a good level of cache.

FACT FILE

Due to shrinking transistor sizes, Gordon Moore (Intel co-founder) predicted that computers would double in processing power every two years in 1975. It has proven to be true and is called Moore's Law.

RAM

Random Access Memory (RAM) helps make the computer quicker to respond to commands. Both RAM and Cache are called primary memory as they are accessed directly by the CPU. Accessing the CPU cache is faster, but it has very limited capacity, RAM is the next quickest option. It is called random access because it can be accessed in any order to help make it fast to use. Measured in terms of capacity in GBs (Giga Bytes) of storage and speed (in MHz). A good desktop's RAM is around 8GB and 2400MHz.

Graphics Processing Unit (GPUs)

One area that you'll see in the details of computer specification and of particular importance to gamers, is GPU (or Graphics Card) performance. These specialised microprocessors manipulate computer graphics to optimally display images, animation and video on monitors or screens. They run at lower clock speeds than CPUs but utilise multiple cores to achieve their goal. A good GPU has 6GB capacity or more for smooth gaming in high definition.

Computer Software

Software ia a set of instructions, data or programmes that enables computers to work and perform specific tasks. They are the non-physical parts that allow the computer to function. Computer software can be split into two main categories. Firstly, we have **System Software** that allows the computer to function. Secondly, there is **Application Software**, that gives users things to use on the computer: the programmes or apps.

Here's a little more detail of what's in each:

System (or Platform) Software

Operating systems (OS)

The OS co-ordinates computer resources and supports applications. Operating systems include Microsoft Windows, macOS and Linux. The OS determines how a computer works and what it works with.

Device drivers

Device drivers connect hardware into the computer system. In this instance, hardware means peripherals, such as printers, mice and displays as well as 'internal' hardware such as graphics and sound cards.

Firmware (also known as embedded software)

Firmware tells devices how they should interact with hardware, allowing them to work. Firmware is permanently embedded into a computer's read-only memory (ROM).

Utilities

Utilities help you analyse, configure, maintain and optimise the computer system, and include disk clean up, file compressing and antivirus software.

Application (or Programming) Software

These are programmes written to allow us to make use of a computer's capabilities. They can be pretty much anything from games and audio apps to database software, spreadsheets and word processors. Here we break them down by the platform they are used on and the way they are accessed. Often the same app can be made in different versions to work across all three of the below:

- **Desktop applications**
  Programmes that use 'traditional' computers with keyboards, including laptops.

- **Web applications**
  Programs accessed on any device through a web browser and linked to the Internet.

- **Smartphone and tablet applications**
  Apps on devices such as the iPhone, Android phones and tablets including the iPad.

Malicious software or malware

A software group on its own, these software 'problems' are more than just a bug or error in written code, they are software programmes deliberately written to damage or spy on other computers. They include viruses, trojans and worms.

The Internet

4.4 billion people use the Internet, that is over half of the world's population. We access the Internet from our phones, tablets, computers and televisions to search for and buy practically anything. We bank our money, gamble, play games, upload and watch video, tell people our thoughts, share our pictures …just to name some of the ways we use it. Most of these online activities didn't even exist when your parents were born. It was only just over 50 years ago (1969) that the idea for Internet began when the American Defence Department's Advanced Research Project Agency Network (called ARPANET) connected a dozen Universities to share information and help accelerate learning with closer collaboration.

The success of ARPANET meant that it grew from the original cluster of 12 to 60 nodes (or computer endpoints) in the 1970s. Other countries started their own sharing networks and linked these between countries in the 1980s, paving the way for the emergence of a global 'Internet' connecting with the United States' non-military version in the late 1980s.

You'll see the "www" at the start of every web address you write and before this http:// or https:// (the extra "s" stands for secure). These abbreviations are now well-known in the Internet world, and these technologies have transformed how we do things, due to the ease of accessing and sharing information (anything!) via computers. A specific language was written called Hypertext Markup Language (HTML) that formats the pages displayed in web browsers. We mention HTML on page 24 in the context of other Internet software and scripting languages.

The Internet provided the communication protocols that allowed computers to communicate over long distances, but it wasn't until 1991 that the first Internet browsing system, called the World Wide Web (WWW), was made available. This system introduced software programmes called web browsers that search for Unique Resource Locators (URL) – meaning digital files and resources on the Internet – that are transferred in Hypertext Transfer Protocol (HTTP) from one location to the next.

Internet Safety

The Internet is a great resource but, like everything in life, there are other people who use it who don't have your interests at heart - even if they say they do. Stay safe and follw the guidelines.

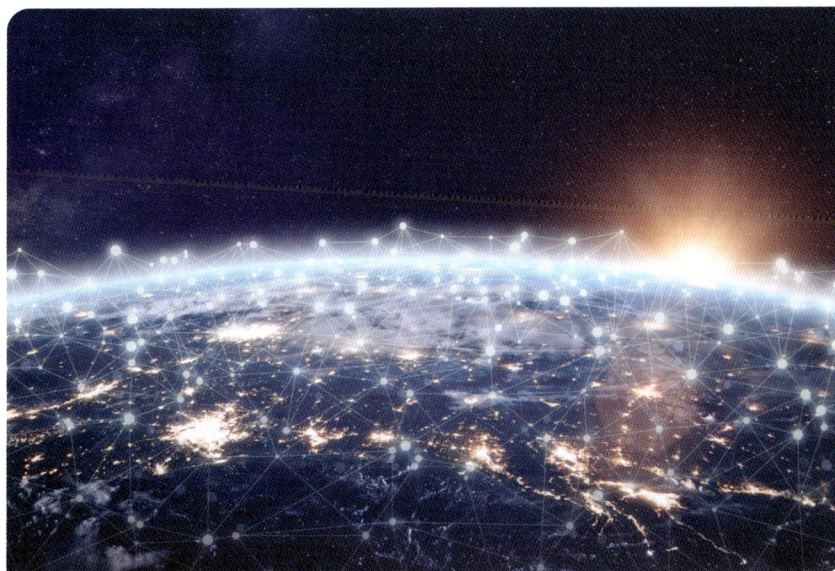

S — SAFE Keep safe by being careful not to give out personal information – such as your full name, email address, phone number, home address, photos or school name – to people you are chatting with online.

m — MEETING Meeting someone you have only been in touch with online can be dangerous. Only do so with your parents' or carers' permission and even then only when they can be present.

a — ACCEPTING Accepting emails, IM messages, or opening files, pictures or texts from people you don't know or trust can lead to problems – they may contain viruses or nasty messages!

r — RELIABLE Information you find on the internet may not be true, or someone online may be lying about who they are.

t — TELL Tell your parent, carer or a trusted adult if someone or something makes you feel uncomfortable or worried, or if you or someone you know is being bullied online.

You can report online abuse to the police at www.thinkuknow.co.uk

Thinking Like a Computer

Humans learn how to do things from a young age by sight and experimentation; as we get older, we learn in a more structured way, with our brains retaining all or a proportion of the information they are given. That's why we practice and get tested on things. A computer doesn't grow up (*have you seen a baby computer?*) so its learning needs to be completely structured.

Computers and robots are given software instructions to process data. In order to understand how computers work, here we try to think of all the steps involved in making a cup of tea. You'd need these steps to programme a tea-making robot. What comes first? What's next? Have you provided all the necessary details? Are they in the correct order?

---

1. Find a cup and a tea bag. Insert tea bag into cup

The robot needs to find these things, does it know what they look like? It wouldn't be any good if the robot found a tea bag and then put it inside a cup and left them both in the cupboard!

---

2. Fill the kettle with water and boil it

Identify the kettle, take it to the sink and open its top. Turn the cold tap on holding the kettle underneath to fill. The water needs to reach above the minimum level - enough for at least 1 cup of tea, not over 'max' before the tap is turned off and kettle carried back to its original position (without spilling the water!). Close the top again. Switch the appropriate switch/push the appropriate button on the kettle (make sure it is plugged into the mains).

---

3. Find a spoon, milk and sugar

The robot needs to find these things, does it open draws and doors to check?

---

4. When the water has boiled pour it into the cup and stir with spoon

Just enough to fill the cup and leave room for milk, when stirring do not go so fast that all the water flies out.

---

5. Remove tea bag, add milk and sugar as required

People can be very particular about the colour of their tea, best check with the drinker if in any doubt.

---

6. Give a final stir, remove the spoon and serve cup to drinker

Hopefully the robot didn't take 15 minutes to make your tea as it wouldn't be hot anymore!

You need to write out the exact steps one by one. Would it work if you changed the sequence, you could probably swap 1 and 2, but others? What if you missed a step out ... what would happen? No water in the kettle, no cup? This is like debugging code – looking to find errors so you can fix them and make it work properly. You could add a lot more detail, for example: the size of the cup, the amount of water and milk, the exact position of items ... can you see others?

As you can tell, even 'simple' activities can have a big list of instructions. Try this yourself with other 'mundane' things like getting into or out of bed, brushing your teeth, putting your shoes on or going to school!

What is programming?

Programming, also called coding, can be simply defined as giving (mainly writing) very specific instructions to a computing or robotic device that allows it to perform a specific task.

Basically, what we just did on the last page. The main difference is, it needs to be in a language that the computer understands. The rest of the book aims to examine four different approaches to coding; these being drag and drop graphics using Scratch, text using Python, 3D gaming graphics using Roblox and through programming robots using **Sphero Edu**.

Each approach has advantages and disadvantages, the idea is you get to try them all and then develop your skills in whichever direction you decide.

> " *Everyone should learn how to programme a computer because it teaches you how to think*
>
> Steve Jobs (co-Founder Apple) "

How computational thinking is taught

The top personality trait identified in software developers is being logical. When you look at what computational thinking is and how it is taught, logic is important. These are the 5 core areas of problem-solving used by computer scientists. You used quite a few of these to help programme the tea-making robot:

Decomposition
Breaking a big problem down into smaller 'digestible' parts

Pattern Recognition
Looking for similarities between and within problems

Generalisation
Adapting solutions from other problems to solve new ones

Abstraction
Taking the detail out of a problem, ignoring irrelevant information

Algorithms
Designing logical steps to follow that solve a problem

Key Programming Languages

Drag & Drop Visual Coding

Built to simplify and help introduce people to coding

Built on Blockly

The top 3 languages used by software developers are JavaScript, Java and Python.

However, all the languages mentioned here are in significant regular use.

Some are platform specific: C# (C sharp) is exclusively for Microsoft, as Objective-C is for Apple

User-side "Front-End" Internet Software

HTML

CSS

JavaScript

 Kotlin

 Java

Mobile Apps

 android

 iOS

 Objective-C

Swift

24

Systems Software

 Objective–C

Desktop Apps

Most software developers working around the world now spend their time working on Internet apps or backend services.

People who can do both front and back-end services are called 'Full stack' developers. Mobile and desktop apps are the next most popular coding projects.

JavaScript

Swift

 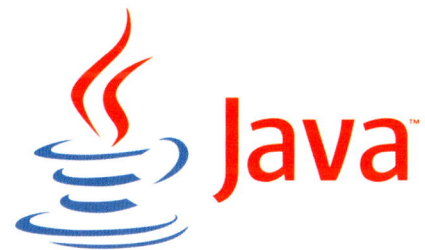

Server-side "Back-End" Internet

Ruby on Rails

php

Most programming languages can only be written on PCs and Macs; however, Scratch and Sphero Edu can be used on phones and tablets too.

Drag and Drop Visual Coding

Scratch from MIT and Blockly from Google are based on the same idea. These programming languages use graphical descriptive blocks of code that can be picked from a list of 'block categories' and moved into place using the left mouse button or a finger on a touchscreen. This process is known as "drag and drop" and is much easier than programming by writing code. Practically anyone can use drag and drop coding, it's perfect for beginners and it's great fun (as well as useful learning) to see the blocks you assemble make things happen on screen.

The blocks conceal the written (text-based) code that allows the computer or web browser to perform the required action. Removing the complexity of writing lines of code also means you shouldn't need to debug it (check for mistakes) due to typing errors.

Please don't think coding like this is just for younger children, though it is beginner friendly. This type of language is used a lot in schools to learn about coding, but it is also used in universities and elsewhere. It helps keep a focus on the 'end goal' of the programming – getting something done, rather than the detail in the syntax and strings that allow the code to be constructed. We introduce syntax and strings in the next section on Python.

It is useful to know and definitely helps as a starting point to other programming languages and methods. Scratch was the first iteration of this type of coding to become internationally popular. Blocky from Google is a similar and alternative block-based coding language. Scratch is most widely used, including in schools, so here we focus only on Scratch.

Getting started with Scratch 3.0

Firstly, you need to be using a device with a web browser. Head to www.scratch.mit.edu and if you haven't got an account already, it's very easy to join, but please check with your parents or teachers first.

Once you're logged in, feel free to have a look around, but probably the best place to start is "Create" – right next to the Scratch logo. This brings you to the heart of the Scratch environment where you can make 'digital stuff' happen on your screen. Clicking 'Create' opens a new project, the next thing to do is to give your project a title. Move your cursor (or touch) the light blue boxed area and type in an appropriate project name here.

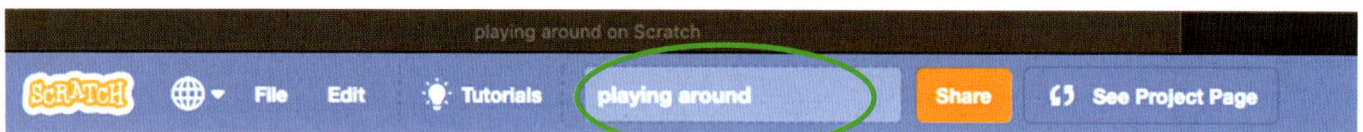

We wrote **playing around**. You might notice that the title of your project also becomes the name of the browser tab you are working on. If you are working online, your project will save automatically, so you can't lose your work. You can also save files to your computer using File>Save to your computer. Now it's time to have a play around!

Sprites and Backdrops

The two core elements of your digital creations on Scratch are called **Sprites** and **Backdrops**. **Sprites** are the *characters* that you can animate to move inside the box on the right-hand side of your screen, known as the **stage**. Backdrops are the **stage's** background. You can have numerous **Sprites**, and these can do pretty much anything in terms of moving and speaking.

The backdrop is the image that sits behind the **Sprites**. It can be pretty much anything, but you only have one of them at a time. As well as choosing from the library of stock images and characters within Scratch, you can also import your own **Sprites** and **Backdrop** from photos or image files you have on your computer.

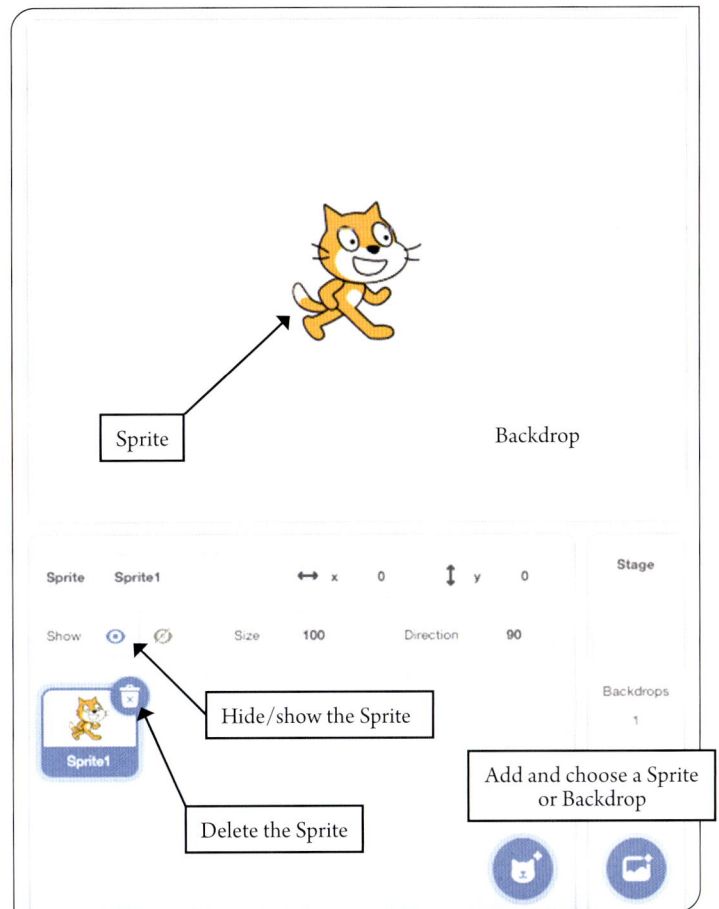

Sprite

Backdrop

Sprite   Sprite1   ↔ x 0   ↕ y 0   Stage

Show ⦿ ⦸   Size 100   Direction 90

Backdrops
1

Hide/show the Sprite

Sprite1

Delete the Sprite

Add and choose a Sprite or Backdrop

Costumes

If you look under the Scratch logo on the left-hand side of the screen, you can see tabs called **Code**, **Costume** and **Sounds**. **Code** is the first tab and is what we will concentrate on through the next pages. Firstly, as we are focusing on appearance, let's take a quick look at **Costume**.

This area is essentially a drawing app. It gives you the ability to create a new **Sprite** from um, ...scratch! It also allows you to modify existing ones. To change the Scratch cat, you need to **Ungroup** the image first to allow you to pick the individual parts you want to change. To make our **Sprite** green we used the **Fill** colour function, picked the colour and then applied it using the *pipette* ✎ feature under **Fill**. You can draw and write practically anything with the **brush, paint, line square, circle** and **text** icons. Try them!

Undo ↰ is always useful to use when you aren't happy with the changes you have made!

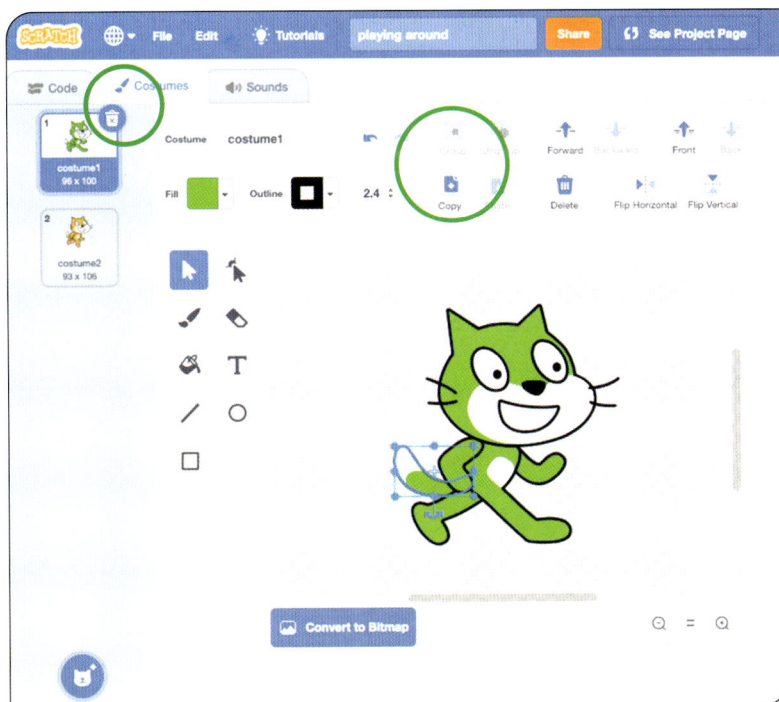

Scratch 3.0

The **Code** tab has everything we need to make digital animations and games. The commands mainly control the **Sprite**, but also relate to the **Backdrop.** There are colour coded areas on the left-hand side that split all the actions into different block categories, these categories are: **Motion, Looks, Sounds, Events, Control, Sensing, Operators, Variables** and **My Blocks**. The blue box with wiggly lines and the add symbol at the bottom clicks through to Scratch extensions – this is where you'll head when you want to push your skills further and link with other internal and external computing capabilities.

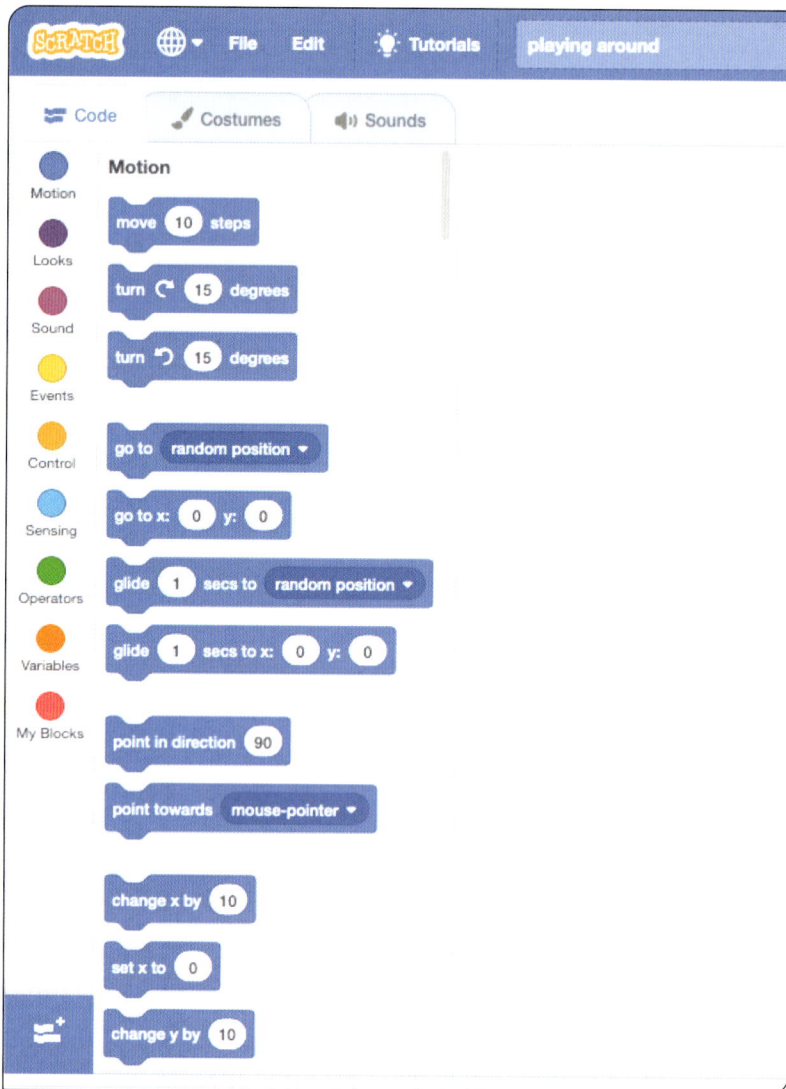

Working on code

Here is your chance to explore the categories and start to code. Firstly, make sure you have the Sprite you want to work with selected by clicking on its box – the one with the delete symbol – but don't delete it!

You can see a transparent copy of the Sprite in the coding window, under the code tab, to check.

Events prompt coding actions to happen. Firstly, you need a start event. Scratch animations are generally started by pressing the green flag, which sits above the **stage** window.

Using **when green flag clicked** is a great way to get your code to run automatically when you start. Alternatively, or more often additionally, you may want the user to interact with your work. If you do, choose **when space key pressed** for example. This is used as a way to interact within games, like moving or shooting.

Motion blocks are all about giving movement to your **Sprite**. The screen is 480 pixels (blocks) wide and 360 pixels tall and you can move your **Sprites** all around it, using positive and negative (e.g. -10) values. The best thing to do is to try the different actions out and link them together using different values.

Looks lets you switch costumes and backdrops, change sizes and add speech in bubbles.

Sound is a must to make your project come alive! Add noises, change volumes, effects etc.

Types of blocks

As you start looking around the different coding blocks, you will notice that most blocks in all categories are **Stack** blocks, which means they are shaped to fit above or below other blocks. Unless they say or you have instructed otherwise, Stack blocks work at the same time as each other.

point in direction 90

Reporter blocks are the other kind of block. These report a value and don't stack but fit into other blocks.

x position

Boolean blocks look like this and are a type of reporter block purely for Boolean values i.e. "1" or "0" or "true" and "false".

Control are a frequently used set of blocks that help give instructions around action duration, repetition and logic. Some of the larger control blocks allow you to insert other blocks inside, like the one here that gives the option of two alternatives. One thing you choose will happen for **if** and another one for **else**.

touching mouse-pointer ?

Sensing blocks ask questions of and detect elements within a project. They help tell the programme when a situation has been met to enable something else to happen. Sensing blocks can be **Stack, Reporter** or **Boolean**.

join apple banana

Operators are calculating blocks, not just for numbers but they can also combine words! These are very helpful when you need maths or conditional questions – known as *logic* – in your animated sequences or games.

set my variable to 0

Variables are created by you to hold a value that can be changeable, like a score in a game. Within Variables, you can make lists. These lists are called *arrays* in other programming languages and can store multiple pieces of information at once, a bit like a shopping list!

My Blocks help if you want to create a function that you can use as many times as you like. You can create your own block with your choice of inputs and text as shown in the image here.

There is a world of Scratch to discover online. First of all, within the Scratch website (www.scratch.mit.edu) itself. There are a lot of tutorials within the site and also around the Internet to help you get to grips with all the digital possibilities this version of visual coding has to offer. Another useful resource is the Scratch Wiki (en.scratch-wiki.info) which is like Scratch's dictionary to help explain Scratch items in more detail.

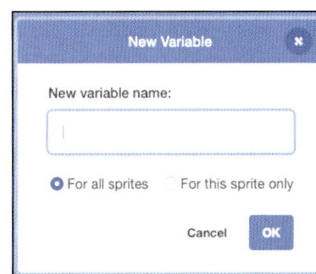

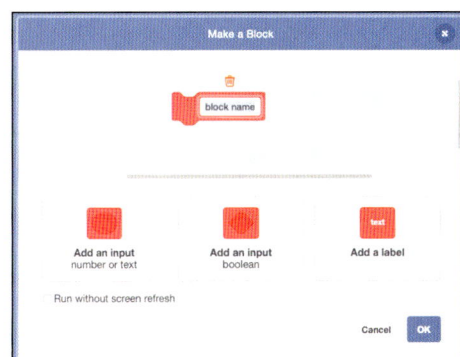

An Introduction to Python

If you want to learn a programming language that goes beyond blocks, the most favoured and powerful text-based language for beginners is Python. Python is easier than most other programming languages to both read and write. Additionally, because Python is open source, there are many libraries that you can access that contain pre-written strings of code that you can freely use to speed up your work. Python is very versatile and can be used across web and game development to desktop apps and scientific applications. It is therefore very worthwhile knowing a little more about it. Let's open it up …

Getting started

To start using Python, first you need to install a programme on your PC or laptop that gives you an environment to develop Python code. These are called Integrated Development Environments (IDE) and exist for all programming languages to help software developers work more quickly. They combine a source code editor (to write and edit code), build automation (to test run) and a debugger. These programmes are compatible with one another and in one convenient place.

Python's own IDE is called "IDLE" named after Eric Idle from the ground-breaking, but now fairly old, comedy programme *Monty Python's Flying Circus*, which was the inspiration for the language name itself. IDLE, and most other programming languages' IDE need a computer or laptop to work, so if it's not yours please ask the owner's permission first. Python's IDLE is free and simple to install, just visit python.org and find 'Downloads'. It should automatically detect which operating system you are using and suggest the appropriate download to click on. If it doesn't automatically give you the option to run, you'll find the downloaded file in your **Downloads** folder, so just click on it and follow the instructions.

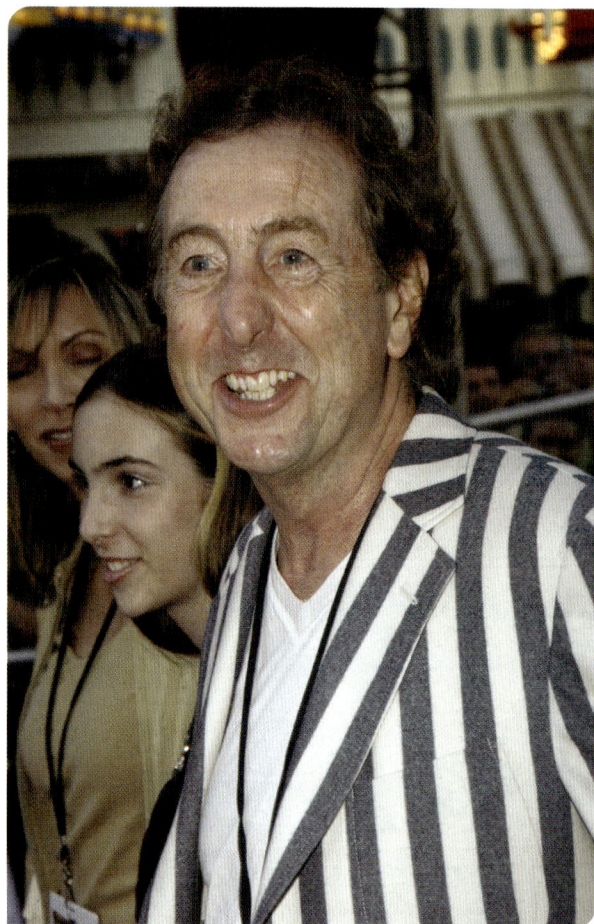

What's in the download?

This image shows the list of items contained within the Python.org download folder.

Name
IDLE
Install Certificates.command
License.rtf
Python Documentation.html
Python Launcher
ReadMe.rtf
Update Shell Profile.command

If you open **IDLE**, you will see a window called **Python** [its version number)] **Shell**. Also known as the Interpreter, this is where the programmes you create and run, are shown.

First command: Print

You can run single lines of code (commands) directly in the shell after the >>> prompt. Let's give that a try. Write a simple calculation, for example, 3 + 5 and then press return. All going well you'll see 8 (or the correct answer to your own calculation).

Now let's display words on the screen. To do this we need the **Print** function and a string. A **string** is data where characters are wrapped in quote marks (" or ') at the start and end.

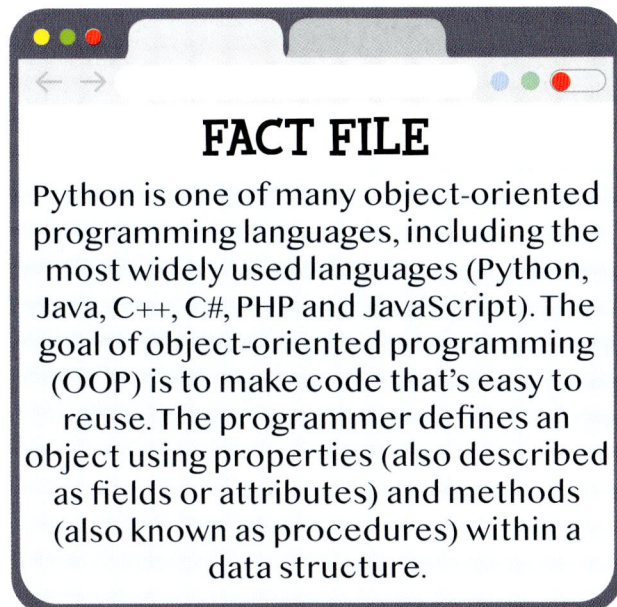

FACT FILE

Python is one of many object-oriented programming languages, including the most widely used languages (Python, Java, C++, C#, PHP and JavaScript). The goal of object-oriented programming (OOP) is to make code that's easy to reuse. The programmer defines an object using properties (also described as fields or attributes) and methods (also known as procedures) within a data structure.

For this next step, after the >>> prompt write: ***print("I am a genius!")*** then press return. You should see **I am a genius!** Notice after you write **print** you need to then use an open bracket (before the quote marks " then write whatever you want to see, followed by the end quote mark " and close bracket). The purpose of the parentheses (brackets) is to execute the function, i.e. to make **print** happen. The quotes around the word you wish to print can be either single ' or double " quotation marks, but they must be matching (**both single** or **both double**).

```
Python 3.8.2 Shell
Python 3.8.2 (v3.8.2:7b3ab5921f, Feb 24 2020, 17:52:18)
[Clang 6.0 (clang-600.0.57)] on darwin
Type "help", "copyright", "credits" or "license()" for more information.
>>> 5+3
8
>>> print("I am a genius!")
I am a genius!
>>> print("I can print anything now – mmmwwwhahahah")
I can print anything now – mmmwwwhahahah
>>>
```

If you're using Windows, you'll see the same results as above – just on a black background.

Files in Python

If you want to write a Python programme with more than one command, you'll need another window. With IDLE open, go to the toolbar, click **File> New File** which will open a new window. You can write the same things we just did for **Print** here and it will work in the same way. The key difference is that you'll have your instructions in the new coding window and the results (what you want to print on screen) appear in the shell window.

Before you can run anything in the Shell window you need to **save** your file. Under **File>**, choose **Save As** (or **Save** if you've already named your file).

CODE	→	SAVE	→	RUN

You'll notice that all Python files end in the **.py** extension, so they should be easy to find. A sensible idea is to create a 'Python files' folder to save them all in.

Errors and debugging

When what you want to happen doesn't happen – congratulations – you have a bug in your code! Perhaps you can try to do things wrong on purpose, just to see what happens … here an error related to the **Print** function.

CODING WINDOW

CODING WINDOW

We wanted **whatever's the matter with you?** to appear in the shell window. However, since we used single and double quotation marks the code hasn't worked, it's not seeing the text after 'whatever'. What we need to write is **print("whatever's the matter with you?")**. Most errors, like this, are easily made; they include typing mistakes, spelling errors or conventions that aren't adhered to; like a missed indentation or not closing parentheses. Training your eyes to see mistakes and understanding error messages are key skills of software developers.

Syntax

In coding, **syntax** is the set of rules for each programming language defining the combination and sequence of symbols that make it work. We received an **Invalid syntax** error as we broke the necessary rules. Python has easier syntax to understand than most other languages.

Variables

Although they look very different, Python commands have many similarities to those used in Scratch. **Variables** are data containers that have names and values that you can change. They are also used in Scratch. The advantage Python has over Scratch and other programming languages, is you don't need a process to create variables, they exist as soon as you put and equals sign (=) between a name and a value. Here's an example using numerical variables with the **Print** function. Give it a try yourself.

● ● ● Python Examples.py **CODING WINDOW** Python Files/Python Examples…

```
a=5
b=3
print (a + b)

|
```

SAVE ➡ **RUN**

```
>>>
======= RESTART: /Users/davidsmee/KICKSUM/Python Files/Python Examples.py ======
8
>>>
```

SHELL WINDOW

We created two variables (**variable a** and **variable b**) and gave them values (**5 and 3**) using an equals sign (=). Then, we used the **Print** function to place those values in a simple sum.

Tip 1: no quotes (" or ') are used in the code when working with numbers. If you put the numbers in quotes, Python then sees them as strings – i.e. words not numbers. If you put quotes around 5 and 3 the answer to (a + b) in the shell window is 53. Tip 2: in order to make the sum work the correct syntax is to use parenthesis around *(your sum)*. Tip 3: variable names must not have any spaces in them, most people use underscore lines _ to act as a space between words.

Printing variable strings

We know from page 31 that we need quotes to assign a string (i.e. text). To output the variable data on the screen, we use print (name of your variable), as we did with the sum previously. This is what that looks like.

● ● ● *Python Examples.py **CODING WINDOW** /Python Files/Python Example…

```
the_variable = "We're starting to learn Python"
print(the_variable)
```

SAVE ➡ **RUN**

```
======= RESTART: /Users/davidsmee/KICKSUM/Python Files/Python Examples.py ======
We're starting to learn Python
>>>
```

SHELL WINDOW

These examples are a great way to start to learn about Python. Try out your own sums, your own strings and when you want more, head online to Python's site and their wiki:

https://wiki.python.org/moin/SimplePrograms. Enjoy unlocking this coding language!

Roblox Studio

Roblox is a fantastically popular gaming environment for anyone 7 years and over. The great thing about Roblox is that you aren't limited to just playing games, you can also create and share games yourself too. In order to do both, you firstly need to have a Roblox account (go to www.roblox.com) and secondly you also need to download the Roblox Studio app on your laptop or PC (www.roblox.com/create) > Start Creating.

Below is the view of Roblox Studio when you first open it. The **All Templates** tab, as you may guess, contains all the templates, meaning everything in both **Themes** as well as **Gameplay**. If you click on **Flat Terrain** (go on, do it!) you will create a flat grass surface in the design window, where you can start adding more elements.

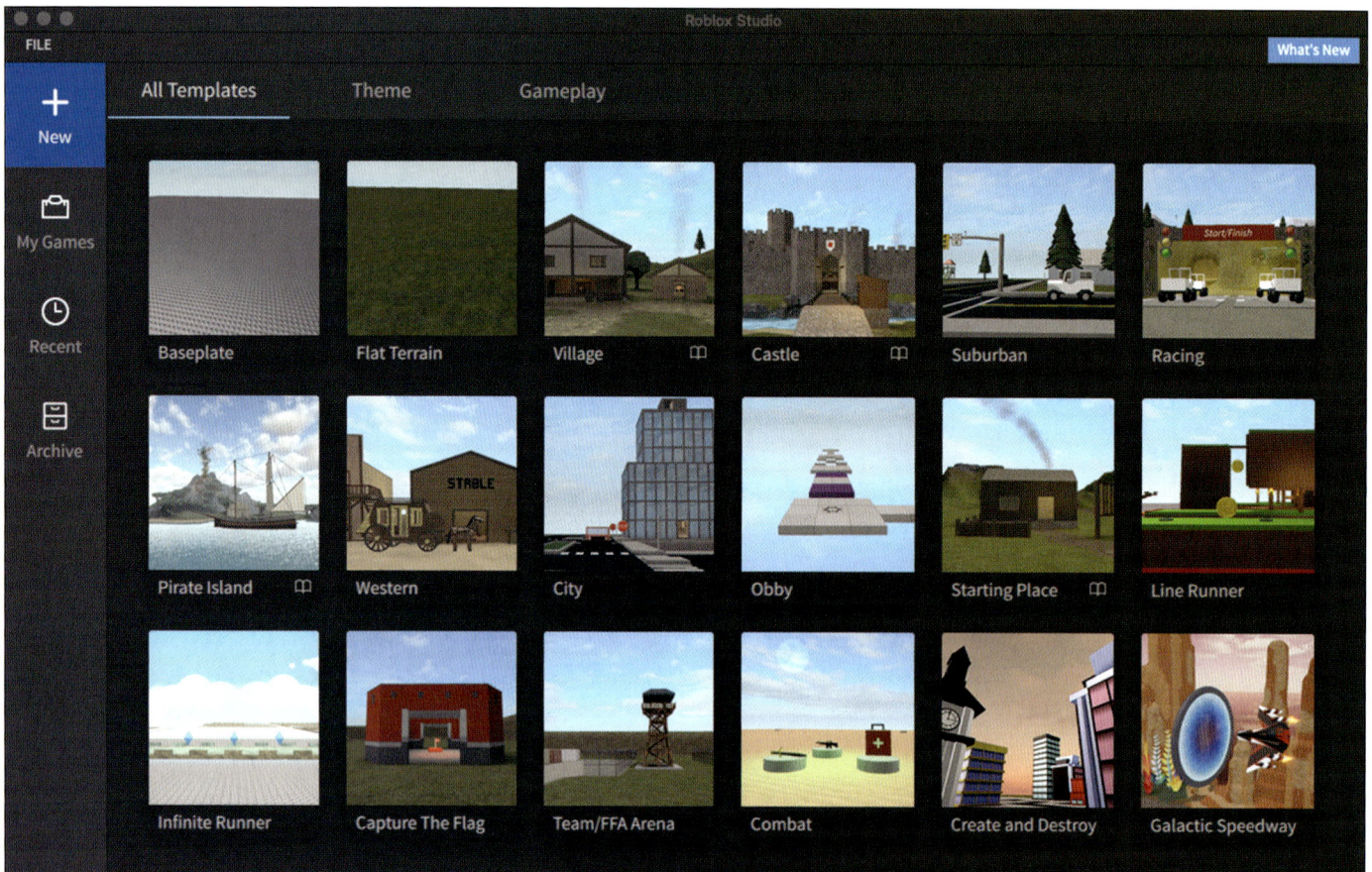

Roblox Studio is a graphical design environment, so when you open a template, this (below) toolbar will be at the top of the screen. Don't panic! We'll talk you through how to start using it here.

To get things started, click on **Part** (circled above) and choose a **Block, Sphere, Wedge** or **Cylinder**. You'll notice that your new part will appear in the exact centre of your viewing window, this can sometimes be a long way away from where you expected it to be, but this will help you learn how to move your view in the Roblox design window (see next page). If you click **Part** more than once it will add more and more of the same part on top of each other. Have fun with adding 3D shapes. It's easy to delete them using backspace or 'undo'.

Test your creations through Play - Playtest

As you create your own Roblox environment it's really important to be able to experience your design as a player would. You do this by pushing **Play** as shown to the right on the toolbar (above). Your Roblox character will spawn in your design window. Use the *now* red coloured square in the toolbar near **Play** called **Stop** to get back to the design mode. Designing in Roblox can involve a lot of trial and error, playtesting your creation allows you to get it exactly as you want it to be for yourself, before you invite others to try it.

Moving around in Roblox Studio

If you are a Roblox player already, you'll find the key controls for movement in **Play** are exactly those used in the game. The game editor window uses the same keys for movement of your viewpoint: **W** is forward, **S** back, **A** left and **D** right. Arrow keys on your keyboard do the same thing and **Shift** changes your camera speed. You use **Q** to elevate and **E** to go down. The **Space Bar** that allows you to jump in-game has no function in design. During design, you can zoom in and out (using the appropriate keyboard shortcuts), and if you hold the right mouse button down you can look 360° around your environment without moving. The View Selector graphic, which looks like a dice, changes the direction of view when clicked on. As you can see in this image, it allows you to toggle around the three axis, x in red, y in green and z in blue, which help you see your work from all angles. **F** makes the camera focus on a single selected part, the **I** key works as it does in-game to focus in on your character and **O** allows you to move the focus out again.

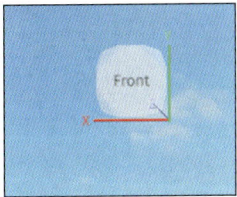

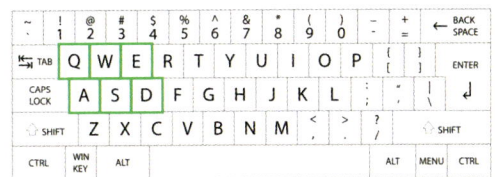

You can change the Laws of Physics

By default, objects in your game act with real-world rules of movement applied. For example, if you put objects freestanding in the air in your design, they'll end up on the ground when you push **PLAY** due to gravity. Also, if you make a sphere it will roll if dropped or pushed. See how this design (left) changed when it was tested (right). The sphere is struck by the long rod and the cylinders fall to the ground. They start to roll, eventually falling over the edge. You can remove the law of gravity in settings to **anchor** objects where you put them in design. We'll find out more about anchors in a couple of pages time.

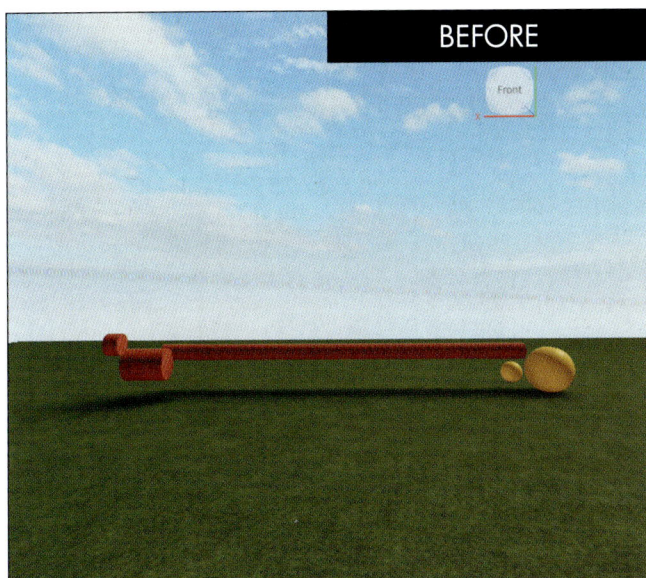

BEFORE

AFTER

Making a Roblox "Obby"

Now you've got some knowledge of the Roblox Studio environment under your belt, it's a good time to begin getting to grips with making and publishing a new game. By following these steps, we'll be able to create our own Obby, which is Roblox language for an obstacle course. Before we do that, head back to the Roblox Studio template screen we showed you on page 34. The quickest way to do this is to delete the screen you are working on (by clicking the cross indicated below). This gets you back to the template screen start point. A notification asks you if you want to save your work.

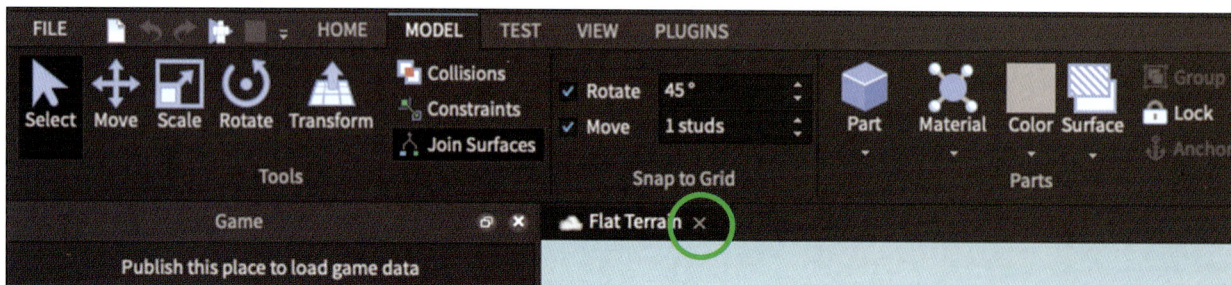

This time instead of **Flat Terrain** select the **Obby** template and you'll open a pretty good initial Obby, with a mix of challenges including hazards to have a **Play** with. By default, you find yourself on the **Home** tab and using the **Select** function. If you select an existing part inside the opened Obby template, you can practice working with it using **Move, Scale** and **Rotate**. Similarly, as you saw in the view selector graphic on the last page, coloured axis lines help give you something to interact with when using these features.

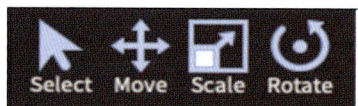

Move: use the mouse to move the part in any direction.

Scale: stretch or contract the size of your **Part**.

Rotate: spin the object around its centre.

If you go to the **Model** tab (next to **Home**) you get a few more options to use that help develop the **Parts** in the obby. Try different types of **Material, Colour** and **Surface**. **Collisions** stop objects from overlapping with each other by making them *solid*. Of course, it may be useful if they do overlap as you can create some great forms by merging different shapes together. The **Rotate** and **Move** tick boxes (not the icons) in **Model**, give you the ability to *snap* the way selected parts are moved (by a varying number of studs) or rotated (in degrees of rotation).

Toolbox

Another feature you'll see and will rush to interact with is the **Toolbox**. It sits in the botttom left of your screen in design view, if you can't find it (and generally to help find things), go to the **VIEW** tab, between **TEST** and **PLUGINS**. The toolbox is an amazing resource to help speed up your design work. On the left of four top level icons in **Toolbox** you can see **Model** and there is a dropdown list here that reveals **Images, Meshes, Audio** and **Plugins** too. Pick anything in here and you'll get a version added into your design window. There are lots of things to choose from including detailed objects, spawn locations and hazards like kill bricks, you can also search for groups of these items in the search box. Have fun, but do remember to pick up where you left off here as we have a few more helpful hints to share with you!

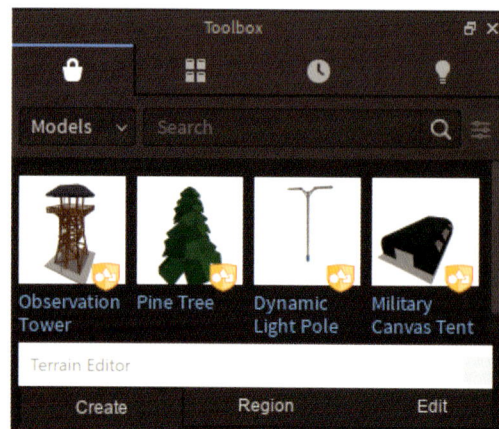

Roblox Studio's Explorer Window

Now you've played around with the functions on the toolbar using the **Obby** template, it's time to start your own project with a blank space. In order to get the blue sky on its own we need to remove all the objects from a template like **Baseplate**. Delete (and save) any open tabs and open **Baseplate** from **All Templates**. The next step is to remove the grey textured surface, which is the only object. To do this you need to erase **Baseplate** from the **Explorer** window view (boxed in green below).

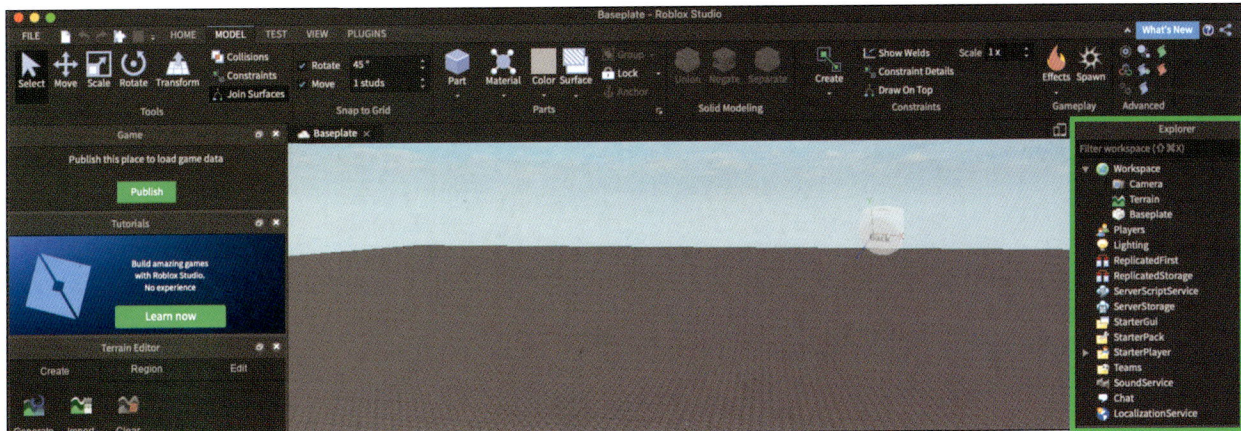

Expand **Workspace** by clicking on it and select **Baseplate** with your mouse, which highlights the text area and then delete it (either *backspace* or click *delete* from the right mouse button options). You should now have endless blue sky – the ideal starting point for an Obby.

Spawn Location

Talking of starting points, in games, you may already know that these are called **Spawn locations**; it's where your character first appears in the game and when you push **Play**. You'll need to add one in your new infinite space to allow you to start a game. **Spawn locations** have a circle in a star appearance (see image below), this one has been colored red. They do exist in **Toolbox**, and you can also add them by clicking on the + symbol on **Workspace** in the **Explorer** window (hover over it with your mouse) and then looking down the long list until you come to **Interaction> SpawnLocation**. It will insert in the centre of your view.

Anchor

Near to your *spawn location*, you'll want to add more parts. These new parts need to be a reachable - jumpable - distance from each other, not too easy nor too difficult to get to. To keep the Obby course entertaining you'll probably have some areas where careful balance is needed over longer thinner parts. To save time across your build you can copy parts either with Ctrl C (the copy sits on top of the original) or Ctrl D (it spawns in exactly the same space). Don't forget to save your progress as you go **FILE>Save/Save as**. One other very important thing to learn before we go any further is *Anchoring*. An **Anchor** makes sure when you put your part in a specific place within your Obby world it stays there – as gravity won't pull it down. You can switch **Anchor** on when you have a part selected, by toggling the toolbar button (next to **Colour**, beneath **Group**) or in the **Explorer** window, under:

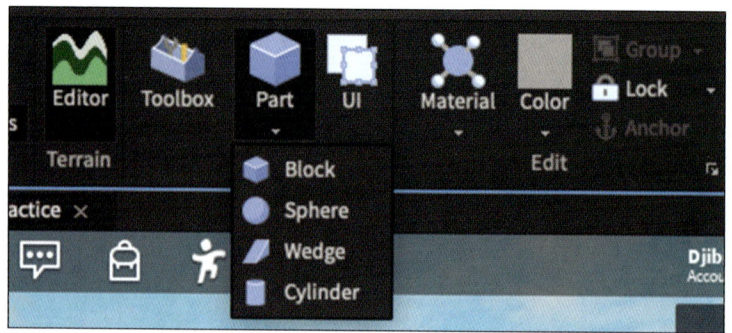

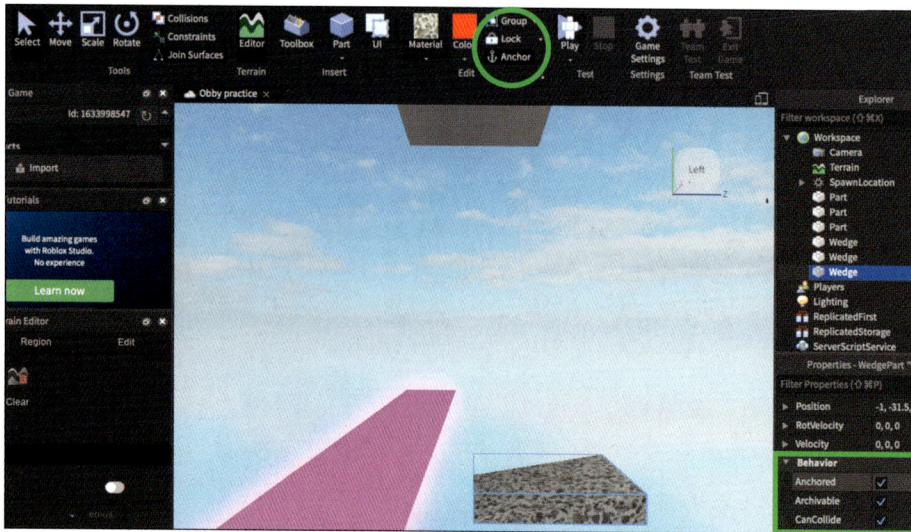

Properties>Behaviour>Anchor.

If you don't see your parts where you expect to see them when you switch from *design* to *play*, a lack of anchor is probably the issue.

Hazards

Hazards add an element of excitement to your Obby as you go beyond the basics. The simplest hazards to master, beyond jumps and thin blocks, are **fall through platforms**. As you might guess, if you jump onto these parts you fall right through them and respawn at the last checkpoint.

The best idea is to help players identify these by making them 'ghost' parts – to do this look at the part's **Properties**, which can be found under the **VIEW** tab or the **Explorer** window. In *Appearance*, go to **Transparency**, set this to **0.3**. Also, in **Properties**, go to **Behaviour**, make sure the part is **Anchored**, then **deselect CanCollide**, so you player can't land on it. Then play it.

Other hazards like kill blocks can be made from scratch, but for now we'd suggest picking ones that have been made in advance from the Toolbox (search: **Kill blocks**).

Beyond the basics

As your Obby gets bigger you will want to start *naming* your parts to more easily identify which is which. You do this by double-clicking the left mouse button on the existing part name in the **Explorer** window and rewrite it with your new name. You can also put different parts into folders to help separate and identify them in groups.

Checkpoints

Other elements to add to your expanding obby are **Checkpoints**. As a player makes their way through the obstacles you've created, they may get caught out by a jump or kill block after progressing for several minutes. It would be very frustrating to respawn from the course start point each time, so you need checkpoints at sensible intervals through your Obby.

You can add checkpoints in a number of ways including the **Toolbox**, but we will focus on another simple way, which is through the **Explorer** window. Either create or choose a part that feels a sensible point in your course for your first checkpoint – change its name to "Checkpoint 1". Then right-click on that part name and select '**Insert Object**' and a long list of menu items will appear. Select **SpawnLocation**, under *Interaction*. This will create an additional part marked with a circle in a star that you will need to **Move** to work with your "Checkpoint 1" part.

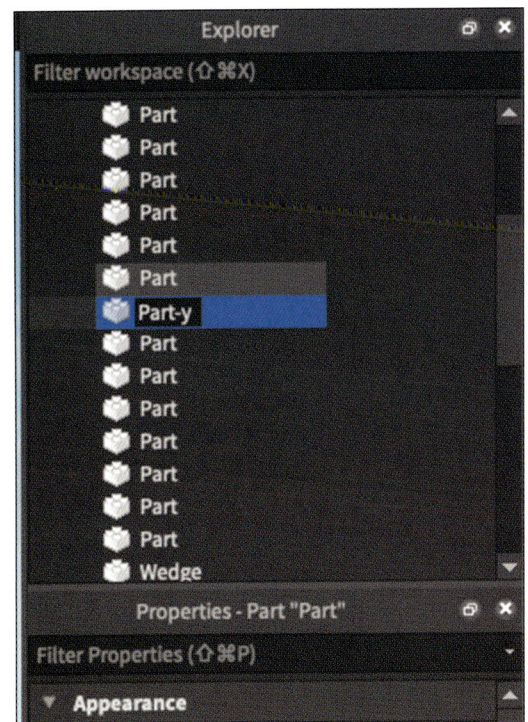

Publish

Once you have a number of anchored parts and other additions with your preferred material and colour, play tested to your satisfaction, it might be a good time to save and publish your first Obby.

Publish to Roblox is again found on the **FILE** menu (the same as **Save/Save as**). This stores your game on the Roblox servers and means anyone can play it if you want them to (by selecting *public*) or you can keep it to yourself (*private*). Give it a name that makes others interested to try it and also know what to expect! A screenshot of your game can be added to give a useful visual impression.

To tell you friends about your Obby use the share icon found on the top right-hand side of the Studio toolbar.

You can spend hours with the knowledge on the past pages and create some great Obbys, and there are numerous different templates, landscapes, styles of game with lots of tricks and traps. You can go deeper into coding by starting to write script in Lua Programming inside Roblox Studio. We hope we've helped get you started; you should head to **developer.roblox.com** when you want to learn more.

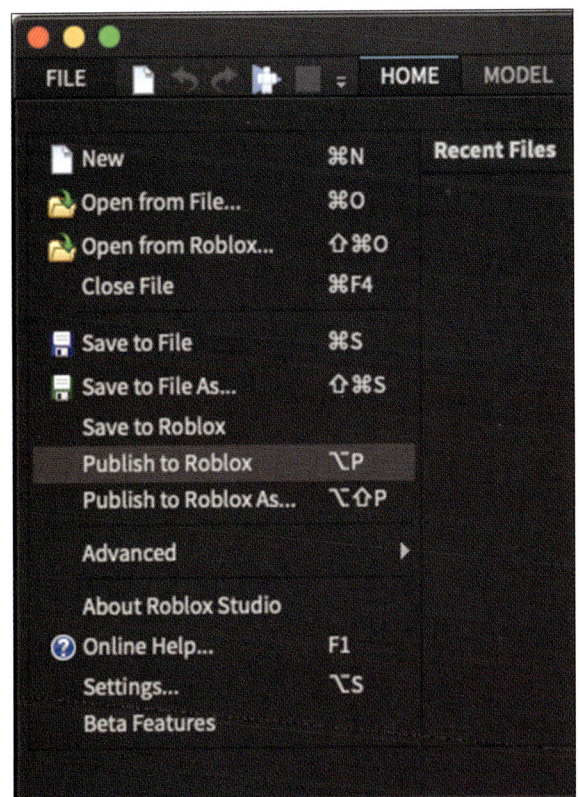

Coding with Robots

Over the last pages we've introduced a variety of entry points to start coding; visual coding with Scratch, Python's text-based coding and Roblox Studio, which lets you create graphics in a 3D-game environment. Another different approach to learning coding and computational thinking and one that offers a multitude of options to suit a wide range of ages, abilities and aims, is robotics.

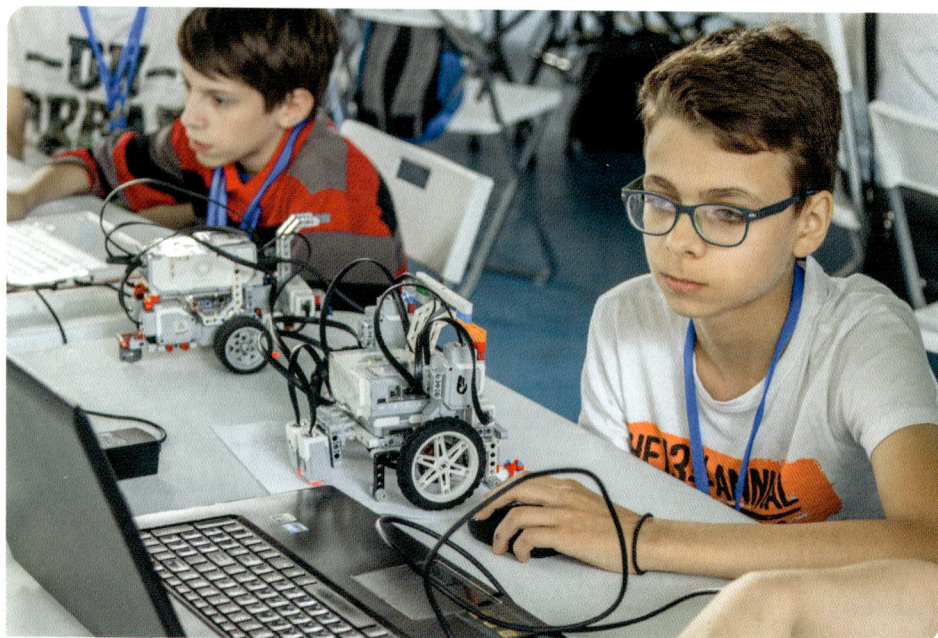

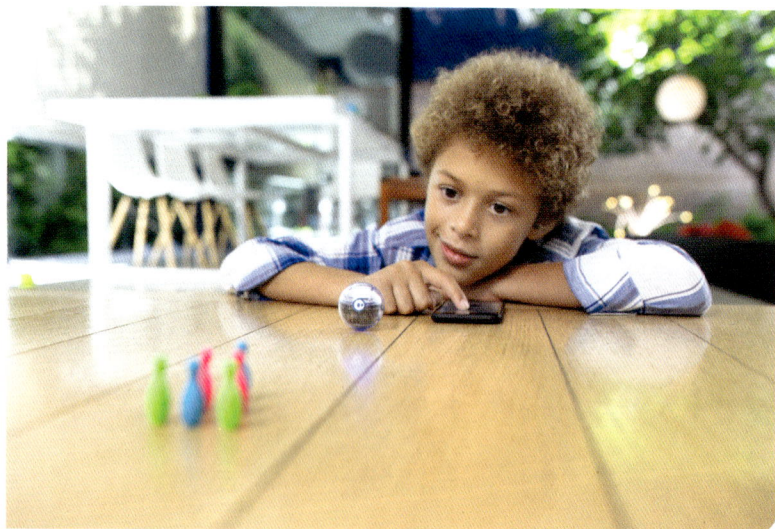

There are many coding robots available to buy from numerous manufacturers. You need to look for robots that are compatible with a) **your set up**; meaning your smartphone, tablet or computer and b) **your coding needs**; for example, do you want to learn more about block coding, Python or JavaScript? It's also got to be something you'd enjoy playing with. Many will offer more than one programming language and ideally, they allow you to compare one language with another to help you progress through from one to the next more easily.

Sphero

Probably the most widely used educational robots come from a company called Sphero. The company name, as you might guess, is associated with the shape of their robots, which started out as smart phone-controlled balls in 2010. Although they now supply a range of different products these days, their spherical ones remain very popular. The company offers their programmable robots with supporting software to make STEM activities and coding more fun to do. To help us examine Sphero coding robots in more detail, we will focus on the functionality within their versatile and even submersible current robot, the Bolt.

The Sphero Bolt

When you get a Sphero Bolt, it'll probably need two things, firstly a charge on the charging base and secondly, an app to control and programme it. Sphero offer a free mobile app called Play available on iOS, Android and Fire OS. They also have a free learning focused app called **Edu** (pronounced E.D.U.) also as a Mobile app, as well as Desktop apps on Windows, MacOS and Chrome OS.

Controlling the Sphero through the apps

Both the **Play** and the **Edu** app offer Drive modes, which give you remote control of the Bolt's movement and speed. The **Play** app has a number of different Drive modes, we enjoyed tilting our phone to move the Bolt. There is also a nice introduction to simple block programming here. **Play** also has games where you can use the Bolt as a hand-held controller, so it definitely lives up to its billing and gives you lots to play with.

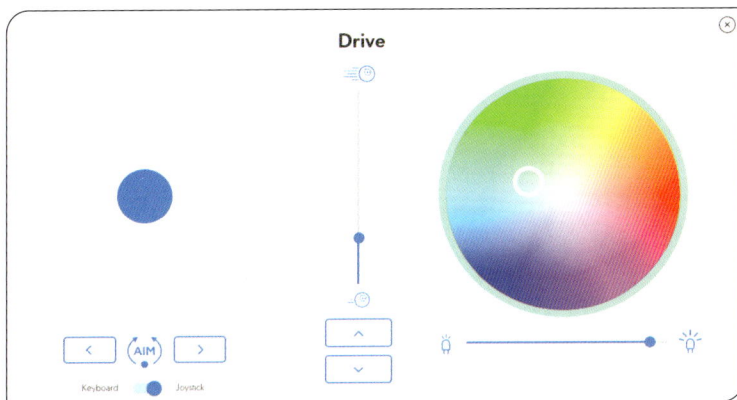

The Edu app

A more focused Drive mode can also be found on the **Edu** app (see image above).

On the left, the small blue circle within a grey one is a Joystick, giving you fingertip (or mouse) control to engage the motors and direct the ball. You can also switch from Joystick to use the WSAD keys on your keyboard to navigate your Bolt around. One thing to try is to create an obstacle course, or perhaps you naturally have obstacle courses around you if you don't tidy up your bedroon so much!

The vertical sliding control in the centre adjusts the ball speed and, on the right-hand side, you can adjust the colours on Bolt's 8x8 matrix LED. Under the colour circle, you can see a horizontal slider to adjust the brightness of the LED, going from dark to light. The features in this graphical box highlight the main programmable aspects on the Bolt that you will be using over the next pages.

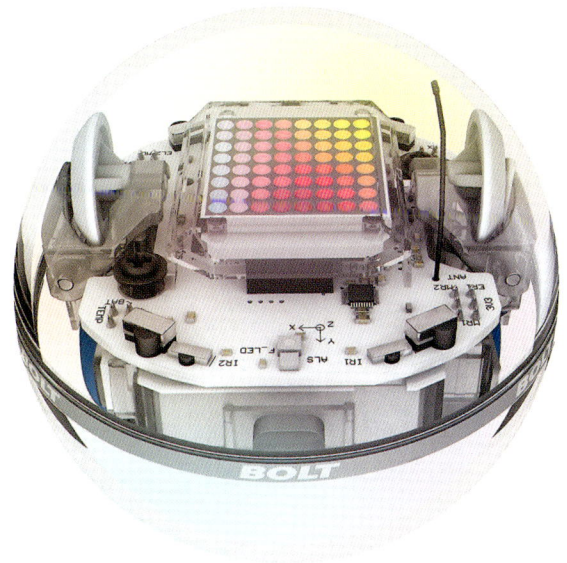

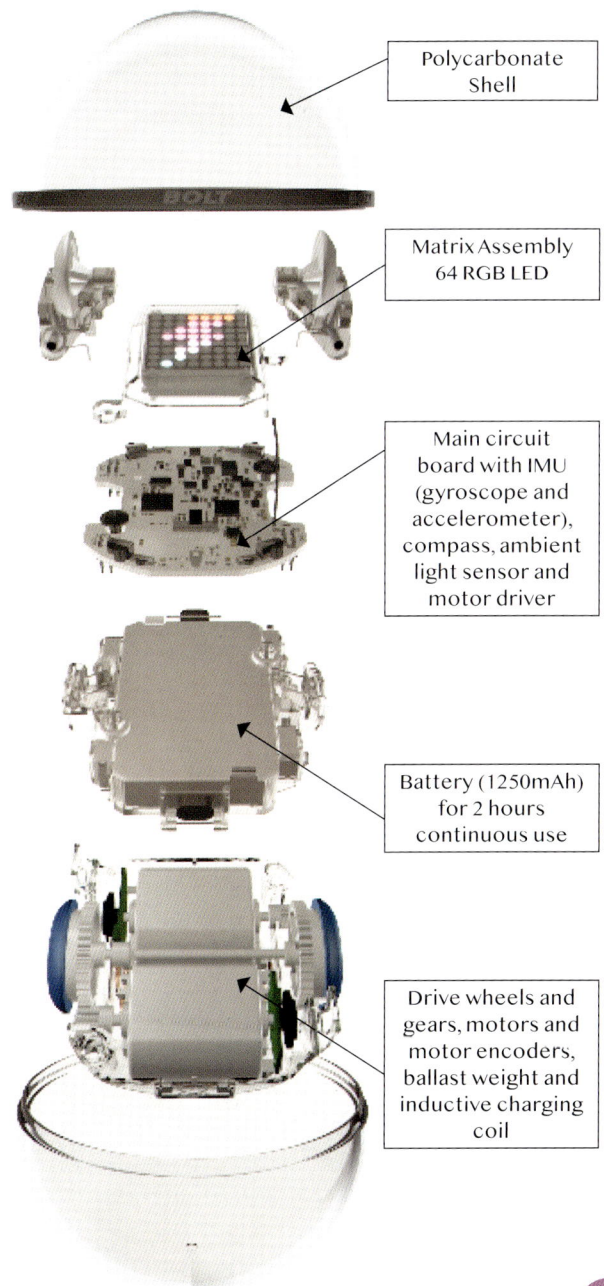

Polycarbonate Shell

Matrix Assembly 64 RGB LED

Main circuit board with IMU (gyroscope and accelerometer), compass, ambient light sensor and motor driver

Battery (1250mAh) for 2 hours continuous use

Drive wheels and gears, motors and motor encoders, ballast weight and inductive charging coil

Draw – coding with a difference

Sphero gives you three ways to code their robots through the **Edu** app. The first one to try is the **Draw** canvas and you get to it most easily through **Programs> + Create** on the toolbar at the top or bottom of your screen. The **Create a Program** pop up allows you to name your programme whatever you choose, then select **Draw** as your programme type and choose the robots you'd like it to work with (for us it's the Bolt).

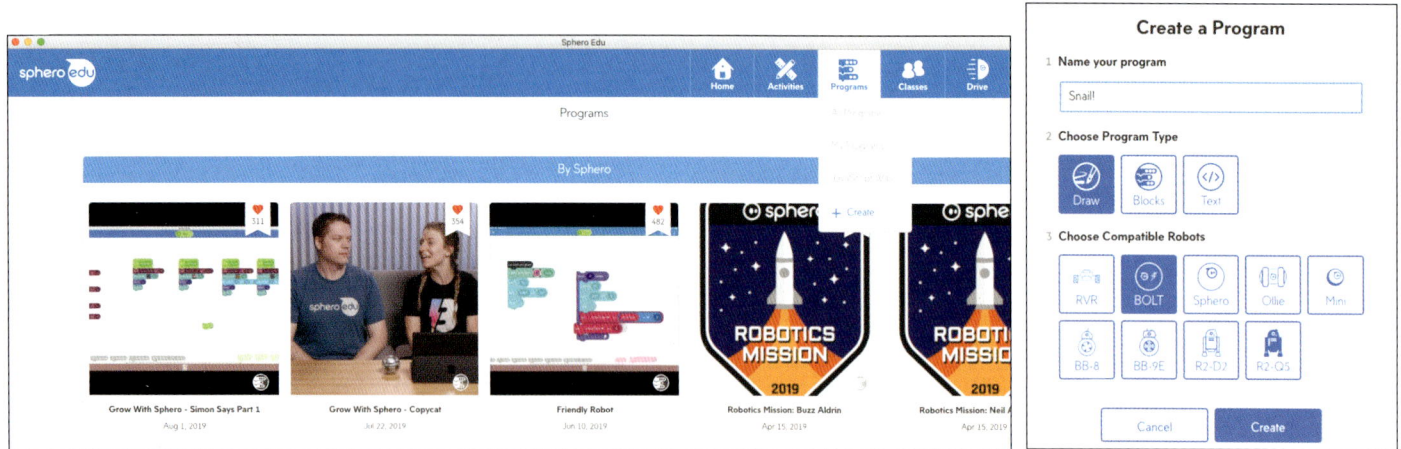

Click create and you have a blank canvas that you can draw on. Your finger (or mouse button) drawings translate to movement of your robot in the directions you used to create your lines and shapes.

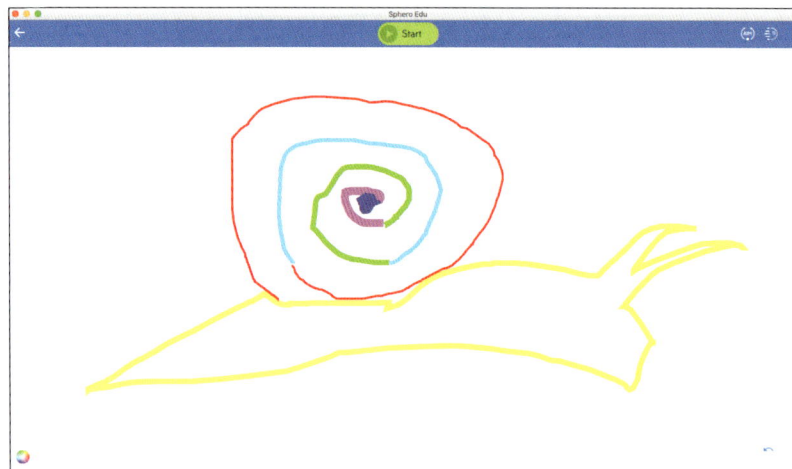

You can also adjust the colour of the LED and change the speed of your Bolt as it moves through the image. A slower moving Bolt is shown in the image with thinner lines.

We made a colourful snail, which starts with the yellow body and then spins into the middle with a range of colours on the LED. We've got a fast speed for the body, and changing speeds for the shell. It's easy to get started and you soon understand how your drawings relate to the movement of your Bolt in front of you. You will need a big space for a full page drawing. When you are finished push the arrow in the top left corner of your screen and your work is saved.

You can make real-world drawings out of your pictures too (though not necessarily with the colour you've drawn on the canvas). Sphero Bolts are waterproof, so you can dip them in paints and let them paint out your picture in real life, be careful not to do this on your Mum's best carpet. Prefer pens, crayons or pencils? No problem. You can create a drawing system based on putting a cup over your Bolt and attaching pens to it with elastic bands. A bit like this **Edu** image. There are an incredible number of projects and ideas that both Sphero and other users (*Community*) have made, freely available to you in the app.

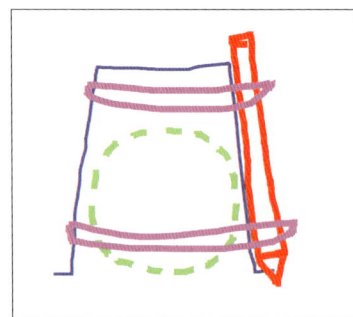

Sphero Blocks

The great thing about coding robots is that there are very practical challenges that you can give yourself to solve in code. Sphero has been working with teachers and schools, so a lot of the needs of international curriculums are included in their projects. They make schoolwork fun, but you can concentrate on pure fun in the projects you create by yourself.

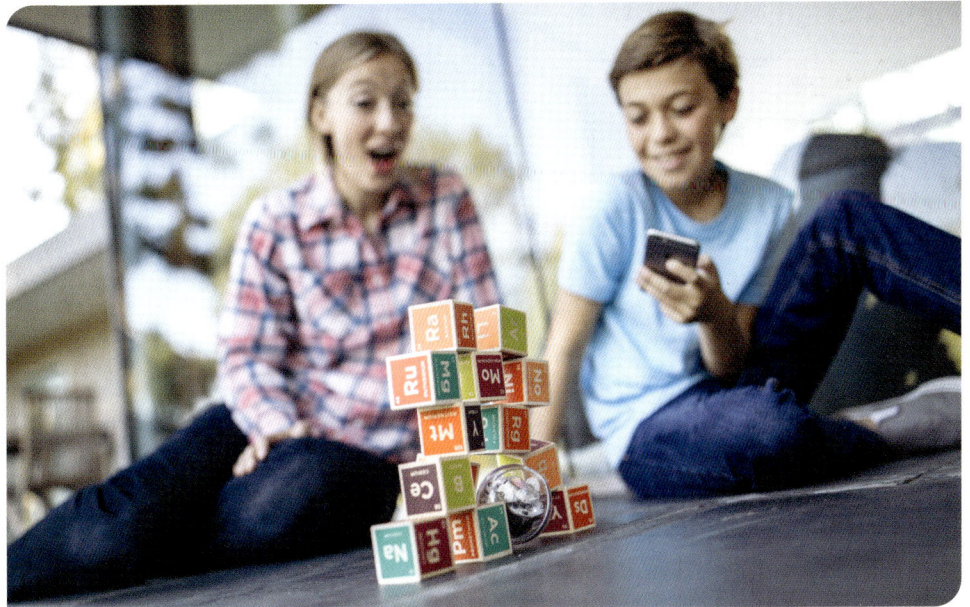

Draw gave us a chance to understand the basic features we can use in coding and – let's face it – have fun drawing and writing things (like our name in joined-up writing) for the robot to follow. However, **Blocks** is Sphero's version of MIT's Scratch where you get to learn intermediate and some advanced principals of coding. Blocks isn't exactly the same as Scratch though because Sphero's programming needs to be specific to and relevant for controlling its robots. Therefore, you'll have an advantage if you've already used Scratch, but there will also be new things to learn and enjoy, especially as you now have control over a physical object.

Categories

Here are the categories you'll find at the bottom of your Blocks canvas:

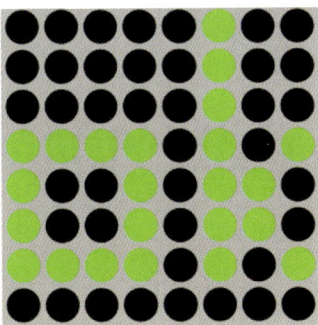

| Movements | Lights | Sounds | Controls | Operators | Comparators | Sensors | Communications | Events | Variables | Functions |

Once you look through the categories, you'll start to appreciate the breadth of function – and therefore opportunities to code – within Sphero. The Bolt gives a lot of extra options over its other robots with its extra features, most obviously its 8x8 square LED matrix. You can create any sequence within the matrix to add personalised patterns and messages – there are also stock ideas from Sphero's **Edu** library to use too.

The infrared connection means that one Bolt can talk to and control other Bolts. Another thing we haven't mentioned is that Spheros can speak! It uses your connected device's speakers to open up a lot of possibilities using sounds and voices (see the purple block code on the right as an example).

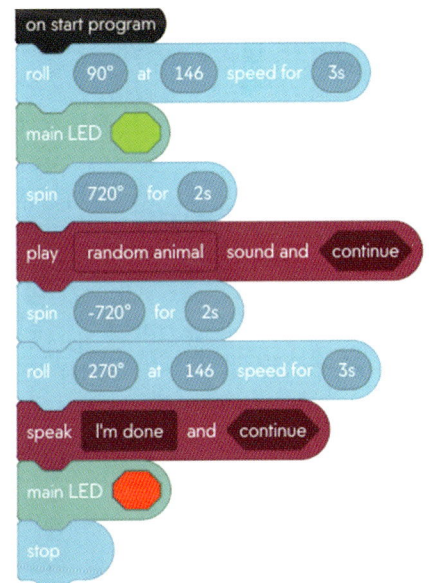

on start program

roll 90° at 146 speed for 3s

main LED

spin 720° for 2s

play random animal sound and continue

spin -720° for 2s

roll 270° at 146 speed for 3s

speak I'm done and continue

main LED

stop

JavaScript for Sphero

One great feature of the Sphero robot range is the ability to progress through different languages. Additionally, when you are working in **Draw** or **Blocks** if you want to dig deeper, there is a lot of additional information to explain exactly how the robot is behaving. You can access **Sensor Data** via the three dots in the top right-hand corner of your canvas. Also hidden behind the dots is the option to read your **Draw** or **Blocks** programme in **JavaScript Code**.

JavaScript

The most popular programming language currently in use is JavaScript. It is hugely versatile (as seen on pages 24 and 25) and pops up **everywhere**. However, it's most commonly found within online forms and generally on interactive websites. JavaScript, when combined with HTML and CSS makes websites more user-friendly and dynamic. Most web browsers have JavaScript interpreters built-in, so pages you find on the Internet (or make) will run JavaScript code automatically.

Sphero allows you to take the knowledge of how the robot works learnt through **Draw** and **Blocks** and uses this reference to gain key knowledge of this very powerful text-based scripting language. You can take your understanding of the robots capabilities and then write programmes for them in JavaScript (**Text**). There is quite a big difference in terms of skills, so this isn't something for beginners. Once mastered though JavaScript is a language in huge demand. If you feel ready for the challenge, I suggest you head to Sphero's JavaScript Wiki: **https://sphero.docsapp.io** where they take you through starting up and getting more involved in the language to control Sphero's robot balls!

Coding for Robotics

In order to code robotics hardware, Python and C++ are probably the most useful languages to learn. However, you can use JavaScript and a number of other languages if you want to.

It is good to get started with any of the programming languages you find here. You'll find most give you skills that are transferable across and useful to work with other languages you might need in the future.

Computing and coding in the future

This book is an up-to-date view of what's happening in computers and coding, but the world of technology around computing changes very rapidly. You yourself are best placed to meet the demands of the future by getting to grips with and keeping pace with technology as you and it improve alongside each other. In 1949 computing science legend John Von Neumann, (who we mentioned on page 17) thought we had reached "the limits of what it is possible to achieve with computer technology". The Manchester Baby in 1948 had a CPU speed of just over 1000 instructions per second, so processors over 1GHz today (most processors) are over a million times better. Even geniuses don't get it right all the time!

FACT FILE

Quantum computing uses quantum bits or qubits. Normal bits have to have a value of either 0 or 1, qubits, on the other hand, can be 0, 1 or both values simultaneously. This creates new possibilities for processing at hard to imagine speeds.

Silicon, the core material used within most electronics today, has about reached the upper limits of its capability to increase processor speeds. This is why microprocessor suppliers have focused on parallel CPU systems (cores) to help increase speeds, but other materials and switches are needed to take us further forward.

Quantum computing might be the way we'll get there. Google and NASA have already announced a quantum computer that's 100 million times faster than typical PCs! Other materials in the frame to succeed silicon are carbon and graphene. If we assume Moore's Law continues, we can expect to have processors with speeds of 5,000,000 GHz (5 petahertz) by 2050.

The last 20 years have seen huge changes in our lives, mainly related to mobile computing and the Internet, that were very hard to accurately predict. It is difficult to imagine, but exciting to think of the prospects that these new processor speeds, alongside advances in artificial intelligence (AI), robotics and other technologies will give us to improve and alter the possibilities in our future on Earth, and perhaps beyond it.

We've already headed out of this world, literally, with robots and computers supporting space exploration. As we can enjoy web cams to see wild animals in Africa today, similarly we'll be able to watch planets and stars that we've never seen before. The real world will be augmented with digital information all around us, perhaps even with computers implanted within us. What do you want 2050 to look like?

What Next?

This book was a useful starting point to learn coding and improve your computing knowledge. It's up to you how you choose to progress. We suggest you attempt new things in the programming languages of your choice, seek out tutorials and opportunities to learn online and in books like this.